"Me, I grabbed a song."

–Frank Sinatra

Ouida,

Remember when Sinatra grabbed you and gave you a kiss at 416 Brazilian P.B. long time ago. When he came to see the 23 King Charles Cavaliers and then when they (Barbara + Frank) had puppies they gave one to the sitting President Ronald Reagan. T'is fun to Remember. A beginning Birthday Present. Lots of love, Jenny + Kenneth October 2003

"Me, I grabbed a song."

–Frank Sinatra

Forever SINATRA

A Celebration in Words and Images

by

Carl Waldman and Jim Donovan

LEGENDS PRESS
Los Angeles

For Anne Waldman . . . another kind of voice.
C.W.

For my father, who loved the Voice first.
J.D.

An FDC Entertainment Book

LEGENDS PRESS

PUBLISHER
Frank Coffey, FDC Entertainment, Los Angeles, CA

EDITORIAL DIRECTOR
Jim Donovan

COVER AND BOOK DESIGN
Ray Dougela, Raybird Graphics, Marina del Rey, CA

ASSOCIATE EDITOR / PHOTO EDITOR
Colby Allerton

The publisher wishes to thank the partners of North American Broadcasting II, particularly Robert Ely, Russell Parker, David Tootill, Anthony Kalomas and Richard Keoseian. For their professional help, thanks to Kurt Wahlner, John Dawson, Dave Eckstrom, Tom Emmitt, Ed McPherson, Ron Richards and Byron Moldo. And for their support, thanks to Marc Siegel, Brad and Vicky Hale, Tony and Elaine Albany, Brian Blake and Jim Jirikow. Sincere thanks to the pros at R.R. Donnelley, especially Harry Hansard, Steve Moore, Jo Earhart, Mike Bell and Janette Wurm. Special thanks to the gifted photographer Sam Siegel and his wife Stella for their gracious help. And last but *certainly* not least, for their love and endurance, our gratitude to Maggie Begley and Tracy Brown.

Picture credits:

Frank Driggs Collection: 12, 14-15, 22, 30, 33, 34, 35, 37, 40, 41, 44, 45, 46, 47, 49, 54, 60, 61, 62, 65, 69, 70, 72, 95, 97, 106, 112, 113, 121, 135, 198, 213, 230; **Michael Ochs Archives:** cover, back cover, front end sheet, 2, 5, 6, 11, 25, 28, 38, 40, 42, 47, 53, 57, 63, 64, 66, 67, 68, 75, 76, 78, 92, 94, 98, 101, 108, 109, 110, 111, 114, 116, 117, 120, 126, 127, 128, 136, 137, 138, 144, 145, 200, 208, 212, 214, 220, 237, 238, 239; **AP/Wide World Photos:** 19, 26-27, 39, 51, 52, 58-59, 81, 83, 84, 85, 86-87, 88-89, 90, 103, 104-105, 122, 132, 133, 141, 143, 146, 148-149, 171, 172-173, 175, 176, 178, 184, 186, 205, 206, 210, 215, 216-217, 218, 226, 240, 242; **John Dawson:** 17, 43, 77, 96, 124, 129 R, 134, 174, 188, 197; **Tim Snow:** flap, 18, 20, 32, 56, 99, 102, 107, 115, 118-119, 129 L, 121, 139, 150; **Sam Siegel Photography:** 8, 10, 16, 125, 130, 151, 152-153, 154, 155, 156, 158, 160-161, 162, 164-165, 166, 167, 168, 180-181, 182, 187, 189, 190, 191, 192, 193, 194-195, 196, 201, 202, 203, 204, 220, 222, 223, 225, 228, 232-233, 235, 236, back end sheet.

Copyright ©1998 NAB Partners II

ISBN: 0-9668136-0-X
Printed in the United States of America

10 9 8 7 6 5 4 3 2 1

Frank and Max Steiner rehearse with the New York Philharmonic
for a show at Lewisohn Stadium on August 3, 1943.

Contents

Forever Sinatra

Appendix

Introduction
The Voice

"You will be my song ..."

The Voice...

The moniker came from a journalist early in Frank's career who shortened the phrase "The Voice That Thrilled Millions," used in marketing by an advertising agency. The label fit perfectly, and it stuck. Why? What made Frank Sinatra such a great singer, such a great musician? The answer's not a simple one. A serendipitous combination of factors made him great—and a fortunate set of circumstances ensured his enduring popularity.

Sinatra's singing is about tradition. Frank combined the tradition of crooners such as Bing Crosby with that of jazz singers such as Billie Holliday and Mabel Mercer. He brought together the emotion of the blues and the smoothness of pop—and then added the energy of a fresh approach to music called swing.

His singing is about innovation. Frank developed a unique style that became the new standard in popular singing. His elegant phrasing influenced countless singers over the next sixty years, and his subtle, more casual delivery contrasted sharply with the over-the-top, near-operatic style of most previous popular singers.

His singing is about taste. Frank was an interpreter. He took the ballads of the great popular songwriters—George and Ira Gershwin, Cole Porter, Irving Berlin, Sammy Cahn, James Van Heusen, Johnny Burke, Jerome Kern, Oscar Hammerstein, Richard Rodgers, Lorenz Hart, Alec Wilder, E. Y. Harburg, Arthur Schwartz, Johnny Mercer, Harold Arlen, and Duke Ellington, to name some of the most prominent composers and lyricists—and made them his own, codifying the American songbook. He worked with the top orchestrators and arrangers of his day, men like Axel Stordahl, George Siravo, Nelson Riddle, Billy May, Neal Hefti, Gordon Jenkins, Robert Farnon, Don Costa, Claus Ogerman, Johnny Mandel, and Quincy Jones, and with them he helped raise the standard of American popular music to lofty heights.

His singing is about attitude, and the attitude is paradoxical. It is tough, but at the same time vulnerable; it is confident, even smug at times, but compassionate; it is nonchalant but committed; it is direct and urgent, but all-embracing and timeless. And no one could deliver the heartbreak of a lost love like Sinatra, who became a "Method" singer: he took the tumultuous romances of his personal life and used them to summon depths of feeling no one else could. The intimate results were breathtaking, heartbreaking, and unforgettable.

His singing is about telling a story. In many of his greatest song performances, Frank became a character progressing through a series of emotions. Each note held meaning— and romance was at the heart of that meaning. Every song was a tone-poem, a glimpse into the heart of a man who had lived and loved and won and lost.

His singing is about joy—the sheer delight of a man who has just discovered he's in love with a woman. He's got her under his skin, he gets a kick out of her, and nice 'n' easy does it. Come dance with me, he says. The unadulterated exuberance of Sinatra's swingin' sessions is unequalled in modern pop.

Frank's singing is about imagination. His listeners imagine they know him. He becomes every man for them. They project their fantasies upon him. He becomes for them a supreme lover, or a success story living the high life, a tortured soul wrestling with his demons, or a contented family man. He creates images and takes his listeners on flights of fancy, and his supreme gift was that he made the listener believe them.

Frank's music is also about a man and his life, and his evolution from crooner to jazz singer to true original, a song interpreter with a unique and inimitable style. His voice became richer in texture as he got older, his readings more natural and believable. When age began to take an effect on his capabilities, he made use of syncopation and phrasing more to tell his musical stories. Even in his late seventies, when that incredible voice had long since deserted him, Frank could be an effective singer.

Left: The most popular singer in America, 1943.

Overleaf: Sinatra recording "Two in Love" with Tommy Dorsey at RCA-Victor Studios in New York City August 19, 1941.

His singing is about hard work. Frank paid his dues. He started young and performed in whatever venue he could find, and always sought out other talent to study. During his time with the Harry James and Tommy Dorsey swing bands, he learned from instrumentalists as well as fellow singers. He sought ways to better himself, such as exercising and holding his breath under water. He took diction lessons. He performed daily vocal exercises.

His singing is about technical ability. Frank learned how to use a microphone for both power and intimacy. He knew how to use it to express an entire range of feeling. With a microphone, Frank could heighten intensity by holding soft notes.

His singing is about perfection. Frank was obsessive about getting the material right in the studio, recording tracks again and again. And he accepted nothing less than the highest professionalism from his collaborators.

His singing is about breath control. From trombone player Dorsey, Frank learned the technique of circular breathing—taking small breaths out of the side of his mouth. As a result, instead of singing two or four bars, he could deliver six or eight seamlessly.

His singing is about phrasing—using rhythm, dynamics, and diction to shape songs his special way. Modern popular song phrasing virtually began with Sinatra. His impeccable sense of timing maximized a song's drama. He shaded notes and embroidered melodies. He made vowels sound crystal clear, while extending consonants. His inflection made a song sound as if he were speaking it as well as singing it, creating an intimate naturalness that was unparalleled and irrestistible.

His singing is about emotion. Frank sang from the heart, the words resonating with personal feeling and conviction. Since it sounded as if he meant what he sang, the music goes from Frank's heart right to the listener's heart. As he became older and wiser—and wearier—it's clear he did mean what he sang. Especially during his classic series of concept albums for Capitol in the fifties, he wore his heart on his sleeve. No popular singer revealed more of his feelings through his music, and it helped make the songs he sang immortal.

Yet Frank Sinatra was more than just the greatest popular singer of the century. He was a peerless performer. Onstage, he came off as relaxed and easygoing, but he was deeply engaged when it counted. He used subtlety to work a crowd—a look, a half-smile, a tremor of the lower lip. Humor was involved, too: he could make an audience laugh with a self-deprecating remark to loosen them up, an off-the-cuff joke that let his listeners feel as if they were his bar buddies, swapping stories with the guy on a stool next to them. But he always maintained complete control of an audience, from the moment he walked from the wings through the crowd until his final encore.

Frank Sinatra was a consummate actor as well as a singer and performer. The camera loved him just as the microphone did, and he had a magnetism that came across onscreen. His sense of timing, with an expression, a gesture, or in dialogue, was comparable to his musical senseof timing. His apparent effortlessness and understated style, developed by years of dedicated work, made us believe the characters he portrayed; his magnetism made even the knockoff, we're-just-doing-this-for-the-hell-of-it films watchable.

Frank's movie characters are open and accessible to us. They are all Frank, and at the same time they are all the different people he played. We know Chip in *On the Town*; we fear for Private Angelo Maggio in *From Here to Eternity*; we despise John Baron in *Suddenly*; we suffer with Frankie Machine in *The Man with the Golden Arm*; we buy into Bennett Marco's worst fears in *The Manchurian Candidate;* and we recognize ourselves in Joe Leland in *The Detective*.

On the smaller TV screen, Frank's charm also came through, whether ad-libbing with fellow performers or in a practiced skit. Frank came across as the genuine article—altogether human, with real emotions. He was having fun, and his attitude was contagious. He didn't achieve the same long-term success on the tube as he had on the silver screen or on records, but that was due more to his reluctance to commit to the medium full-time than any intrinsic weakness in his TV appeal.

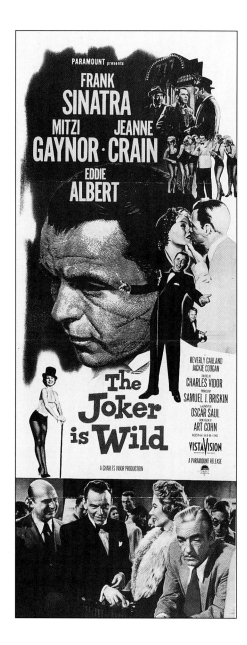

Right: Sinatra and his boyhood idol, Bing Crosby, perform "Well, Did You Evah?" in *High Society* (1956).

Sinatra gave us more than great music, performances, and roles. He gave us a way of thinking about ourselves, a philosophy of behavior and style. In his choice of songs and his interpretation of them, as well as in his passionate real-life romances, he showed us that men could be manly and romantic at the same time—that one could project machismo while expressing his innermost romantic feelings. Through the vicissitudes of his career and relationships, and his courage and endurance in the face of stacked odds, he also showed us that an idol could be simultaneously grandiose and vulnerable. Through his reputation as a creature of the night, he showed us the energy and romance of the dark hours as well as the suffering—we know he has seen the world through the bottom of a glass and has paid dearly for his sins. Perhaps no other man suffered so openly, so revealingly, and on such a public stage as Sinatra during his torch singing in the fifties. He made it acceptable for a man to show his emotions. If Frank could do it, why couldn't we? He anticipated the new "caring male" of the latter half of the twentieth century, complete with the irreconcilable complexities in every man.

The music that is Sinatra … the vision that is Sinatra … the man who is Sinatra … will never die.

Forever Sinatra.

Body and Soul

Hoboken Dreams

"I'm all for you body and soul . . ."

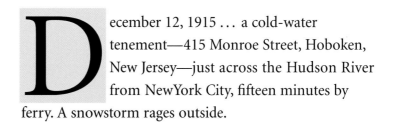

December 12, 1915 … a cold-water tenement—415 Monroe Street, Hoboken, New Jersey—just across the Hudson River from New York City, fifteen minutes by ferry. A snowstorm rages outside.

The mother, diminutive twenty-year-old Natalie Catherine Garavente Sinatra, known as Dolly, had wanted a girl. But now she was relieved the touch-and-go forceps delivery of this thirteen-pound baby is over and successful. All present had feared the worst—stillbirth—until Dolly's resourceful mother Rose, with experience as a midwife, had doused the boy with cold water, to which he had responded. Now relief … and pride. The father, twenty-three-year-old Anthony Martin Sinatra, known as Marty, was proud to have a son and a bruiser at that. These Italian immigrants, Marty, born in Sicily to a family of grape growers, and Dolly, born in Genoa to a family of educated lithographers, had high hopes. In this country called America, the newborn might just turn out to be an engineer.

A name for the boy? Francis Albert Sinatra—Frank, after a good friend of Marty's, a local Irish newspaperman named Frank Garrick. There would be a lot of nicknames to follow.

It was a tough town and a tough neighborhood, but a supportive family. In the first decades of the twentieth century the Italians were at the bottom of the social ladder, beneath the Germans, many of them merchants, and the Irish, who controlled the police and fire departments. But the Sinatras were upwardly mobile.

Blond, blue-eyed, outspoken, and occasionally foul-mouthed, Dolly worked at a number of jobs, including midwife (and abortionist, which the family tried to hide in later years), candy maker, and barmaid, but it was her work as a Democratic ward leader that opened doors. She was good at it, consistently delivering five hundred votes for the party machine at election times and even pretending to be Irish when it helped get things done. She saw to it that her husband Marty—more quiet and passive, and less likely to push for favors—got a job at the Hoboken Fire Department as fireman and part-time cook.

He was no slacker. His other jobs had been a boilermaker at a shipyard and an extra in movies. He also did some boxing as "Marty O'Brien" to appeal to the Irish fight crowds. The saloon they eventually purchased at Fourth and Jefferson they named Marty O'Brien's. To some people in the neighborhoods, the Sinatras were the O'Briens.

The family eventually moved out of the tenements—first, in 1927, to Hoboken's Park Avenue. Five years later, in the midst of the Depression, they purchased a three-story, four-bedroom dream house on Garden Street.

After the difficult birth, ninety-pound Dolly couldn't have any more children, so she and Marty treated their only child like royalty. They provided well for him; the little boy with the big blue eyes got everything he needed. But they were so busy that little Frank was often in the care of his grandmother Rose and aunts Mary and Rosalie, and sometimes an elderly Jewish woman by the name of Mrs. Golden. As an adolescent, he had a lot of freedom, hanging with boys on street corners, sneaking off with girls, sitting on the waterfront, and gazing at the Manhattan skyline. Young Frank learned to take care of himself on the streets, enduring several boyhood fights. And if he couldn't handle the bullies himself, friends who appreciated his company, and his generosity—little Frank always had extra money to treat his friends to ice cream and sodas—did. The skinny kid with big ears and scars on his cheek, ear, and neck from the forceps—"Scarface," other kids called him—dreamed of becoming a prizefighter as his father briefly had been.

Through all these years, Frank never looked like a poor boy. Early on, Dolly dressed him in Little Lord Fauntleroy-style suits. Later, she set up a charge account for him at a local department store. His extensive wardrobe, fedora included, led to the nickname "Slacksy O'Brien." He even had access to a car—a green 1929 Chrysler without a top that he had bought for twenty dollars—at age fifteen.

"I wanted a girl and bought a lot of pink clothes. When Frank was born, I didn't care. I dressed him in pink anyway. Later, I got my mother to make him Lord Fauntleroy suits."

–Dolly Sinatra

Previous page: The artist at age five.

Right: Stylish even at an early age.

Overleaf: Martin and Dolly Sinatra, 1963.

Above: As a teenager, Sinatra poses with a pipe
a la Bing Crosby, his idol.

Frank was a smooth talker, and with his intense blue eyes and disarming smile he generally had his way with girls. Once he achieved any intimacy with them, he figured he had rights to them forever. Many of them felt the same way.

He didn't have his way with teachers, though. Frank was a restless student. School would not be his road to riches. He attended Hoboken's David E. Rue Jr. High School from 1928-30, after which he enrolled in A. J. Demarest High School. Most reports have it that he dropped out (or was expelled for rowdiness, according to Frank himself) a couple of months into his first (sophomore) year. He attended Drake Business School for a semester as a way to fulfill a New Jersey statute on compulsory education for children under sixteen.

In any case, as a young adult, Frank worked a number of blue-collar jobs, including catching rivets and cleaning condenser units at Jersey shipyards, and unloading crates of books in New York City. A short-lived job in 1932 was bundling and unloading delivery trucks for the *Jersey Observer* local afternoon newspaper, where his godfather Frank Garrick was circulation manager. Frank didn't keep the eleven-dollar-a-week job very long, either. When a young sportswriter died suddenly, he presumed he could step into the job without proper training or even asking anyone for help. He rubbed Garrick's boss the wrong way and was let go instantly.

But something else lured him. Something else had caught his imagination during his boyhood and fueled his dreams—music.

"The struggle of the infant would shape the character and conduct of the boy and remain a motivating force in the man."

–Nancy Sinatra

All the Way

The Rise to Fame

"Who knows where the road
will lead us . . ."

Frank Sinatra couldn't read music. But he sure could hear it. And he could express it. He learned his artistry, not from lessons, but by paying attention to others and doing it himself. No successful entertainer more embodies the phrase "where there's a will there's a way." At least in the early days Frank made it in show business through sheer willpower.

The phonograph and the radio provided the early stuff of dreams for young Frank. Rudy Vallee with his megaphone had been all the rage. Will Osborne picked up a megaphone too. Gene Austin had the hit "My Blue Heaven." Russ Columbo sang "Prisoner of Love." The Happiness Boys also inspired him. But it was Bing Crosby who became Frank's number-one idol. Frank even wore a white hat with a gold anchor on it and smoked a pipe like Crosby, whose smooth style was revolutionary in popular music.

Growing up, Frank sang at his parent's social events—as early as age eleven to a player piano. He'd sing on street corners with friends to the accompaniment of a ukulele, given to him by an uncle. After dropping out of school, he sought out every chance he could to sing with bands. Early on, he sang through a small megaphone like Rudy Vallee, but he learned to caress the microphone more and more. To further his art, Frank went to Manhattan music stores, made friends with countermen and cajoled free sheet music out of them in order to learn the lyrics of the latest hits.

At first, his parents didn't like the idea of his becoming a musician. Dolly blew her famous temper when she first spotted pictures of Bing Crosby on his wall. She still had dreams of Frank going to college. But she began to believe like Frank believed, and in 1932 she lent him the sixty-five dollars for a public-address system and money for sheet music. The twenty-dollar car to get to gigs was the other essential piece of equipment. She also lined up work for him at Democratic Party meetings. Frank played school dances and clubs and neighborhood theater amateur shows with a variety of accompanists. He would rent out his sound system and his sheet music to local bands if they let him sing with them. Nobody in Hoboken thought he was much of a singer (a friend even refused to let him sing at her wedding), but nothing discouraged him. And all the while he was honing his craft.

Frank got further inspiration in the summer of 1935 on seeing Bing Crosby live at the Loew's Journal Square in Jersey City. After hearing the crooner, he told his date Nancy Barbato (who would become his wife) that he would be as famous as Crosby one day.

The next few years, Frank haunted Manhattan radio stations and music spots, many of them around 52nd Street. The area was his trade school. The Onyx Club … Jimmy Ryan's … The Famous Door … Leon & Eddie's … The Hickory House … Tony's Place … Club 18 … these were a few of the clubs the young singer frequented. From singers and musicians such as Mabel Mercer, Billie Holiday, Sarah Vaughan, Fats Waller, and Count Basie he learned his craft, synthesizing what he saw and heard into his approach to interpreting a song. It was great training for a young singer.

In September 1935, at age nineteen, Frank got his first break in the music business, performing for NBC's radio show *Major Bowes and His Original Amateur Hour* (which would eventually become the *Ted Mack Amateur Hour*), broadcast nationally each week from the Capitol Theater in New York City. For the spot, he was teamed with the Three Flashes out of Englewood, New Jersey—Jimmy "Skelly" Petrozelli, Patty "Prince" Principe, and Fred "Tamby" Tamburro. There are varying accounts of how Frank ended up singing with the Three Flashes—that it was Bowes' idea to put them together after they had auditioned separately, or that Frank drove them to gigs and asked to sing with them on learning of their audition, which they turned down until influential Dolly pressured them. In any case, they performed on the *Amateur Hour* as the Hoboken Four, singing together the Mills Brothers' hit "Shine." Audience reaction was positive, and the group received a contract to play a succession of dates as part of Major Bowes' traveling show, doing the vaudeville circuit. Frank also got to sing in two one-reel shorts for Major Bowes that played briefly at Radio City Music Hall; he acted as a waiter in *The Night Club* and as a member of a blackface singing troupe in *The Big Minstrel Act*.

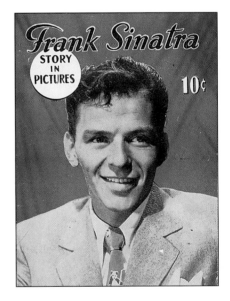

Previous page: Frank with bandleader Raymond Paige at the Paramount Theater, 1944.

Right: American WAVEs surround Frank before a concert at the Paramount in 1941.

FRANK SINATRA

"And then I said, 'Well, anyway, ladies and gentlemen, here he is, Frank Sinatra.' And I thought the damned building was going to cave in. I never heard such a commotion, with people running down to the stage screaming and nearly knocking me off the ramp. All this for a fellow I never heard of."

–Jack Benny

Left: A typical crowd in line for a Sinatra theater appearance in the forties.

Above: Sinatra arriving in Pasadena, California, 1943.

This was a paying gig—Frank earned about sixty-five dollars a week with Bowes—but the group changed their name often to appear to audiences as amateurs, one permutation being The Secaucus Cockamanies. They played as far away from home as Vancouver, Canada. Frank was the lead singer, and his getting most of the audience's attention caused friction within the group. He was homesick anyway, so after about three months he quit and returned to Hoboken.

In 1936, Frank worked the local circuit again, playing Italian weddings, Irish political rallies, social clubs, and Elks Club meetings. At Union Club dances, he was the regular vocalist. Knowing that the new medium of radio had created a new opportunity for singers, offering regional and even national exposure, Frank made a concerted effort to land work. He began performing in a dozen quarter-hour weekly programs broadcast over four local New Jersey radio stations, earning only carfare. He also sang at WNEW radio in Manhattan. Often he performed as filler between scheduled shows—anything for air time.

In early 1937, Frank sang for an NBC radio show (with Dinah Shore at one point), a job arranged by his cousin, Ray Sinatra, who played for the NBC house orchestra. The pay: seventy cents a week. On May 12, 1937, he performed swing music as Frank Sinatra and the Four Sharps on the radio show *Town Hall Tonight*, hosted by Fred Allen.

Ambitious and focused, Frank also worked hard to improve his entertaining skills. Late in 1936, he had started taking diction and voice lessons with a New York vocal coach, John Quinlan, to eliminate his New Jersey accent and improve the lower end of his vocal range. The lessons improved his singing and phrasing tremendously.

Frank's next big break was a roadhouse in Englewood Cliffs, New Jersey—the Rustic Cabin. A local promoter and friend named Hank Sanicola lined up an audition and, once again, in 1938, with Dolly once again pulling some strings, he was hired as a singing waiter. He waited on tables and sang with the Harold Arden house band, eventually emceeing too. He started out at fifteen dollars a week; he later would earn twenty-five. But more important than the dollars was the exposure.

"He was always striving to be better. Learning. Hoping to get on with a bigger band."

–Nancy Barbato Sinatra

36

Above: With Mark Warnow's Hit Parade Orchestra
and Chorus, 1943.

Above: A train was still the primary mode of
transportation for entertainers in the forties.

Right: Bobby-soxers jam the Paramount Theater in
October 1944 to cheer their idol.

And he got it. He soon built a name for himself locally as well as to a radio audience on both sides of the Hudson, since concerts at the Rustic Cabin were broadcast weekly for WNEW's *Saturday Dance Parade*. Frank worked the Rustic Cabin for about a year and a half. While refining his singing style and his stage persona, he kept an eye on the competition, frequenting Manhattan theaters and clubs to hear name performers.

Area musicians often came to the Rustic Cabin— songwriter Cole Porter, for one. (He wasn't overly impressed, he told Sinatra years later.) In the late spring of 1939, Harry James heard him from his hotel room in Manhattan. James, the former trumpet player for Benny Goodman, was looking for a singer to front his own big band, the Music Makers. He showed up with his new female singer, Connie Haines, and, after hearing Frank live, returned the next night and signed him for a two-year contract at seventy-five dollars a week.

Sinatra had been discovered. Now he would be exposed to a national audience. James wanted his name to be Frankie Satin, but Frank (at the insistence of his outraged mother) kept his family name. His first appearance with James was at the Hippodrome Theater in Baltimore on June 30, 1939; he sang "Wishing" and "My Love For You." They also made records together. That July, they recorded "Melancholy Mood" and "From the Bottom of My Heart" for the Brunswick Label, a subsidiary of RCA, and in August, "All or Nothing at All," which four years later would be a big hit for Frank.

Harry James's band never took off like some of the other competing swing bands—Benny Goodman, Glenn Miller, Artie Shaw, Count Basie, Duke Ellington, Bob Crosby, Jimmie Lunceford, and Tommy Dorsey. Frank, looking to rise to the next level, began feeling restless. Trombone player and bandleader Tommy Dorsey had been hearing about James's young singer, and when his popular vocalist in the Pied Pipers, Jack Leonard, began talking of a solo career, Dorsey auditioned Frank in Chicago in December 1939. Frank was asked to sing "Marie" in the Leonard style. He pulled it off, and Dorsey soon offered Frank a long-term

Above: Frank in a publicity shot in the early 1940s.

contract at one hundred dollars a week. There was one condition—he had to get out of his two-year contract with Harry James. When Frank finally worked the nerve up to ask James for his release, James tore up his contract and wished him well. Frank was forever grateful. The talented Dick Haymes took Frank's place.

In January 1940, Sinatra made his first appearances with Tommy Dorsey's band as a featured singer, touring through the Midwest and eventually playing the Paramount in Manhattan in March. On February 1, 1940 , he made his first record with Dorsey and his Pied Pipers: "The Sky Fell Down" backed with "Too Romantic." On May 23, 1940, Frank and Dorsey recorded "I'll Never Smile Again," which soon became a number-one single.

The slender crooner's musical career was snowballing. He was the lead singer in one of the hottest bands in the country, and his singing had improved dramatically, helped in no small part by breath control secrets shared by Tommy Dorsey. With Dorsey and his star-studded band (which included drummer Buddy Rich, trumpeter Bunny Berrigan, and vocalist Jo Stafford), he played concert after concert and made numerous recordings. In May 1941, *Billboard* named him Outstanding Male Vocalist of the Year; by the end of the year, Downbeat followed suit. (He displaced his idol, Bing Crosby, who had held the spot for six years.) Frank also made two film appearances with the Dorsey band-in the 1941 releases Las Vegas Nights and Ship Ahoy. As media attention grew, so did his national following. And as had always been the case, most of his dedicated fans were girls. Because many wore white sox with saddle shoes, they became known in the press as "bobby-soxers." Another term for Frank's devotees were "swooners," for their dramatic reaction to his soulful style.

On January 19, 1942, with Dorsey's blessing, Frank made his first solo recordings: "Night and Day," "The Night We Call It a Day," "The Song Is You," and "Lamplighter's Serenade." Frank performed on a subsidiary of RCA so as not to upset Dorsey. Dorsey's arranger, Alex Stordahl, worked with him, and the results were electrifying. Frank now believed he could pull off a solo career.

"Working in a band was an important part of growing up, musically and as a human being."

—Frank Sinatra

Above: The Harry James Band, Atlantic City, New Jersey, 1939. James is seated, center; Sinatra is on his left.

Left: Frank at the Hollywood Bowl, 1940s.

Above: Sinatra performs with the Crosby kids for
a 1948 radio show.

Right: A forties publicity photo.

The inevitable came—the day when Frank felt he was ready to go it alone. His last tour with Dorsey's band was during the summer of 1942. Dorsey, unlike James, was not so willing to let his star singer go, and he insisted on collecting a share of his earnings for some time; it took a buyout in 1943 to free Frank once and for all. (One version of events has it that certain mob-related friends of Frank's visited Dorsey to convince him to make the deal, though Dorsey, and everyone involved, denies that story.) In a radio broadcast on September 3, Tommy Dorsey announced Frank's departure from the band. From the bandstand Frank introduced his replacement, Dick Haymes—who had also replaced Frank in Harry James's band three years earlier. The skinny kid with the big ears was on his own at last.

Sinatra's first solo appearance came on December 30, 1942, at the Paramount Theater. He performed as an "extra added attraction" with headliner Benny Goodman, the clarinet player known as the "King of Swing." Comedian Jack Benny introduced him, and the young girls in the audience went wild. A few days later, Frank's new press agent for his solo career, George Evans, reportedly hired teenage girls to respond to Frank and to swoon and scream with excitement. The publicity stunt proved superfluous, with hundreds of girls acting out on their own under the spell of the microphone-caressing singer in the floppy bowtie. The original four-week engagement was so successful that it was extended to eight. Frank now made $25,000 instead of $750 a week. He was the most popular singer in the business and among the highest-paid. He was a musician in demand as well as a teen idol, paving the way for Elvis and any number of others in the years to come.

Frank Sinatra had made it all the way from the streets of Hoboken to the top of the entertainment world—just as he'd been telling everyone he would.

Frank Sinatra had a way with women—up close and personal, as well as from the stage. From his earliest days onstage he had been besieged by young female admirers. His blue-eyed gaze was all knowing, his attitude cocksure, his words street-clever; that combined with an aching vulnerability and the smoothest delivery on the planet was like catnip to his bobby-soxers. His singing went right to their hearts, and often enough the rest of their bodies followed.

He had a lot of crushes and girlfriends when young: neighborhood girls Marie Roemer and Marion Brush were two of the teens with whom he was involved in Hoboken. Both became friends with Dolly, who managed to be involved with all that concerned her only son.

In 1934, Frank met the one who would become, both in his mind and his mother's, the best candidate for marriage. That summer, he stayed at his Aunt Josie's (Mrs. Josephine Garavente Monaco) in Long Branch on the Jersey Shore. Frank was eighteen. From the porch of his aunt's house, where he often strummed his ukulele and sang songs, he was taken with a seventeen-year-old, dark-haired, Italian-American beauty across the road—Nancy Carol Barbato. She was spending the summer with her father and aunt and uncle and their families. One day, while she was giving herself a manicure on her porch, he approached her.

One version of events has it that Frank's first words to Barbara were: "Hey, what about me? I could use a manicure." Not an inspired line, but the relationship blossomed anyway into a summer romance and more. Even after he had returned to Hoboken and she to the next town over, Jersey City, they kept seeing each other. It was Nancy who went with him the following summer to see Bing Crosby live at the Loew's Journal Square in Jersey City. Frank wrote poetry to her and talked of his dreams of being a singer and his frustrations at what he was up against. This neighborhood girl from similar background, this "girl next door," supported him in his quest and experienced the early breakthroughs with him—working for Major Bowes, the early radio spots, working at the Rustic Cabin, endlessly hustling for singing gigs on radio, in roadhouses, anywhere. Her father helped him out too, hiring Frank for his plastering business—although he often had to go over Frank's work himself.

All the Things You Are

Nancy … and Marriage

"All that I want in all of this world is you …"

But Frank kept seeing other young women too. The more success he had, the more available were the dalliances. There was another Nancy—Nancy Venturi, with whom he had a relationship with in 1938. The same year, Frank began seeing Toni Francke (Antoinette Della Penta Francke), a twenty-five-year-old from Lodi, New Jersey, while she was separated from her husband. When she claimed she was pregnant, Frank promised to do the right thing; but when Dolly got wind of it she changed her son's mind. Three months later, Toni had a miscarriage, and soon Frank began avoiding her. So she had him detained on a morals charge. Frank was arrested after a performance at the Rustic Cabin for breach of promise on November 27, 1938, and jailed for sixteen hours. The charge was dropped when Frank promised that his mother would apologize to Toni. (The fact that she was already married might also have had something to do with it.) But the apology never came, and three weeks later, on December 22, she accused Frank of committing adultery. This charge was dismissed in open court on January 24, 1939. Frank promised Nancy he'd never be involved with another woman again—one promise in life he wouldn't keep.

Soon afterward, on February 4, 1939, Frank and Nancy were married at Our Lady of Sorrows Church in Jersey City. They drove to North Carolina for a four-day honeymoon. On their return, they settled in a three-room walkup in Jersey City at a monthly rent of forty-two dollars.

That June, Frank signed with Harry James. Nancy, soon with child, joined him on the road. These were the happiest days of his life, she later stated, even though they had to struggle to make ends meet. She cooked for the band. She knitted the floppy bow-ties for Frank that became his trademark. She was his partner, soulmate, confidante, and sounding board.

Their first child, Nancy Sandra, was born on June 8, 1940, in Jersey City. Their second child, born on January 10, 1944, also in Jersey City, was a boy—Franklin Wayne Emmanuel (Frank Jr.). Their third and last child, Christina (Tina), was born on June 20, 1948, in Los Angeles after the family moved west.

We were together twenty-four hours a day-driving from one show to another in our new car- and he was doing what he loved. It was wonderful."

–Nancy Barbato Sinatra

Previous page: Frank and Nancy at a New York City nightclub.

Right: At the 1946 Academy Awards. Frank's Oscar was for *The House I Live In.*

Despite a beautiful home and three beautiful children, life became increasingly difficult for Nancy after the move because of Frank's dalliances. Moreover, she didn't have the same support system she'd had with family and friends in the East. But Nancy remained true to Frank even when he stayed away nights and when she could no longer convince herself that rumors of affairs were just rumors. And she remained a friend to him long after their separation in 1950 and their divorce the following year as a result of his relationship with the actress Ava Gardner.

"I was devastated—just like Mom.

He had left me too."

–Nancy Sinatra

Left: Frank and Nancy leave
a Hollywood nightclub in 1946.

Right: Three-year-old Nancy poses with Dad
and Mom in 1943.

All or Nothing at All

At the Top

"Half a love never appealed to me . . ."

By the early 1940s, Frank Sinatra had become a cultural phenomenon—the Phenomenon, as many spoke of him. His voice was all over the place—on stage, records, and radio. The media reported his every move, coining new words to discuss his impact—"Sinatramania," "Sinatrauma," "Sinatrance," "Sinatritis," "Sonatra," and "Swoonatra," for instance. To his fans, he was most often "Frankie" (or "Frankee") or "the Voice," but countless other names appeared in the press—"The Lean Lark" (in his twenties he weighed only a hundred and thirty pounds), "The Croon Prince of Swing," "The Sultan of Swoon," "Dreamboat," and so on.

Fan clubs sprung up all over. At one time there were more than one thousand, with names like Frankie's United Swooners, The Slaves of Sinatra, The Hotra Sinatra Club, The Bow-tie-dolizers, and even The Flatbush Girls Who Would Lay Down Their Lives For Frank Sinatra Fan Club. Fans couldn't get enough of him and tracked his next record release or his next radio and concert performances. His skinny frame, the blueness of his eyes, the single curl straggling across his forehead, the way he gave a sidelong tremor of his lower lip, or his latest oversize bow-tie— All these became major topics of conversation.

After his eight-week solo run at the Paramount Theater in 1942-43, Frank earned the big money and could live the high life. He didn't flaunt his enormous success in the early years, however. There was a war on. The year before, on December 9, 1941, two days after Pearl Harbor and three days shy of his 26th birthday, Frank was classified 4-F at the Newark Induction Center. The cause was a punctured eardrum, suffered either during his difficult childbirth or during a series of childhood mastoid operations. Frank was sensitive to the fact that some of those young men going off to war resented his exemption. Yet the fact that for many of America's young women he symbolized all those vulnerable young men—the boy next door risking his life for his country—contributed to his success. The fact that many of the other singers were off the scene during the war years didn't hurt, either.

Frank's press agent, George Evans, finessed the public's view of Frank by reinventing his past. He claimed Frank was born in 1917 to make him closer in age to the bobby-soxers; that his parents had been born in the United States; that the family had been hopelessly poor; that Dolly had not been an abortionist, but a Red Cross nurse in World War I; that Frank had survived gang wars in his neighborhood; that he had graduated from high school and had been a star in sports; and that he had worked as a sports reporter. He also covered up Frank's love affairs and painted him as a dedicated family man. The mythology created around Frank perhaps helped make him more palatable to parents concerned with their daughters' obsession with Frank, or to critics who wanted to dismiss American popular music, but it was Frank's talent and charm that won over an ever-expanding audience and drove his career.

In February 1943, Frank made his first feature film without the Dorsey band— Columbia Pictures' *Reveille with Beverly*. It was a cameo spot during which he sang his hit "Night and Day." That same month, he began making regular appearances on the popular CBS radio show *Your Hit Parade*, a weekly countdown of the ten most popular songs sponsored by Lucky Strike. Through 1945, he sang on other CBS radio programs as well—*Reflections, Broadway Band Box, Max Factor Presents Frank Sinatra, Old Gold Presents Songs by Sinatra*. And he also would have his own regular show, *The Frank Sinatra Show*, on CBS from January 1944 to June 1947. During this heyday of radio, Frank dominated the airwaves with live appearances as well as hit single releases.

In March 1943, Frank signed with Columbia Records. It had cost him $60,000 to resolve his contract with Dorsey. Frank's new talent agency, MCA (his former agency was Rockwell-O'Keefe) put up $35,000; Columbia, at the urging of Manie Sachs, director of A&R (Artists and Repertoire), lent Frank $25,000 as an advance against royalties. Because of a strike by the musicians' union, he couldn't yet go in the studio with an orchestra, so Columbia re-issued "All or Nothing at All," recorded with Harry James in 1939. It became Frank's first million-seller. Frank participated in his first solo recordings with Columbia on June 3, 1943, including "You'll Never Know," "Close to You," and "People Will Say We're in Love." At this session, because of the ongoing strike, he recorded a cappella with the Bobby Tucker Singers.

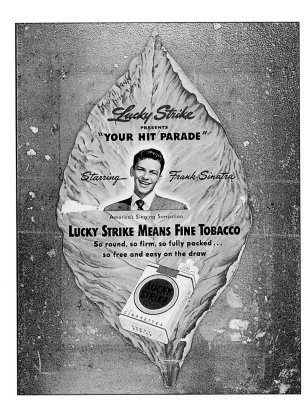

Previous page: Sinatra and arranger Alex Stordahl at Columbia Records, 1944.

Overleaf: Sinatra, Frances Langford, and Bing Crosby rehearse for the 1945 Command Performance by the Armed Forces Radio Service.

The list of Frank's venues were expanding. In March 1943, he performed at the Riobamba in Manhattan, his first solo nightclub appearance, in an attempt to win over a more mature audience. The public embraced him, and the media response was overwhelmingly positive. Within a week he went from promising singer to national sensation. That summer he played with the Cleveland Philharmonic, the Philadelphia Philharmonic, and the Los Angeles Philharmonic. In October, he played the Wedgwood Room of Manhattan's Waldorf-Astoria Hotel, perhaps the toniest supper club in America. Each engagement was enormously successful. Older audiences now understood more and more the power of his music and stage personality.

In September 1943, Frank signed a seven-picture deal with Radio-Keith-Orpheum (RKO) Pictures. *Higher and Higher* was released that December, with Frank singing five songs. The following February, he signed a five-year deal for one-and-a-half-million dollars with Metro-Goldwyn-Mayer (MGM) Pictures.

For some time, Frank, Nancy, and little Nancy (who had been born in 1940) had lived in the East. They had moved into a seven-room brick house at 220 Lawrence Avenue in Hasbrouck Heights, New Jersey. But with Frank's second career as a movie actor, it now made sense for the family to be in California. With their new child, Frank Jr. (born the January before), the family moved to the West Coast in the spring of 1944, traveling by train. At first they stayed at the Castle Argyle in Hollywood, then moved to 10051 Valley Spring Lane in Toluca Lake in the San Fernando Valley near Bob and Dolores Hope. (The Sinatras would eventually buy a $250,000 home in Holmby Hills and build a $150,000 compound in Palm Springs as well.)

Frank started filming his first MGM project, *Anchors Aweigh*, co-starring Gene Kelly, in June 1944; it was released the following August. Then life really got busy for Frank.

Linton Weil's
Riobamba
151 E. 57th ST.
WALTER O'KEEFE
SHEILA BARRETT
SPECIALLY ADDED
First Cafe Appearance
FRANK SINATRA
His voice has thrilled millions
Russell Patterson's
Magazine Cover Girls
BRANDWYNNE'S MUSIC
CHAVEZ and His
Rhumbas

Complete Revue
for *DINNER* at 8
Then at 12 and 2:30 A.M.
Res: Fred Chiaventone
PLaza 8-1960

"I get an audience involved, personally involved in a song—because I'm involved myself. It's not something I do deliberately; I can't help myself.

If the song is a lament at the loss of love, I get an ache in my gut, feel the loss myself and I cry out the loneliness, the hurt and the pain that I feel."

–Frank Sinatra

Above: Frank's first solo nightclub appearance,
at the Riobamba in Manhattan in March 1943.

Above: A signed photo of the Harry James Band, Hotel Sherman, Chicago 1939. Frank is seated at center.

"The eyes are blue and direct, like northern crystals of ice."

–Jonathan Schwartz

Above: Sinatra in 1938 with Major Edward Bowes,
whose *Original Amateur Hour* gave him his first
big break in 1935.

Above: Sinatra with Martin Block,
a popular disc jockey, in 1943.

In September 1944, Frank visited the White House and met President Franklin Delano Roosevelt, whom he idolized. The meeting received front-page coverage. In October, Frank once again began an engagement at the Paramount Theater in Manhattan, his first in seventeen months. When 30,000 fans came to claim only 5,000 seats, a melee ensued which the press dubbed the Columbus Day Riot. In November, with the end of the musicians' strike, Frank recorded nineteen songs for Columbia. In May of the next year, 1945, Frank embarked on a six-week USO tour to North Africa and Italy with comedian Phil Silvers to entertain soldiers just after Germany's surrender. On that trip, Frank met Pope Pius XII. Back in Hollywood, Frank partied with the top celebrities of the day, actors such as Humphrey Bogart and Lauren Bacall.

In September 1945, RKO released *The House I Live In.* Frank, as an Italian-American from a poor neighborhood, was sensitive to the issues of prejudice and classism. He had surmised that, because of his great popularity and influence, he could help enlighten people and had come up with the idea of a movie to spread a positive message. He had convinced participants to donate their time and to relinquish all proceeds to charity. In the ten-minute short, Frank, playing himself, speaks to a group of boys about racial and religious tolerance. In November, Frank did a lecture tour of schools on the subject of civil rights. *The House I Live In* earned Frank a special Oscar at the Academy Awards on March 7, 1946.

By the end of 1946, it was estimated that Frank was recording an average of twenty-four songs per year, enabling Columbia Records to issue a new Sinatra record a month. His records were selling at an annual rate of 10 million. His career was going strong and would continue to thrive in terms of projects and earnings. But the following year, 1947, would see more and more negative publicity and the start of a downward spiral in Frank's personal and professional life.

Blues in the Night

The Dark Ages

*"My mama was right,
there's blues in the night . . ."*

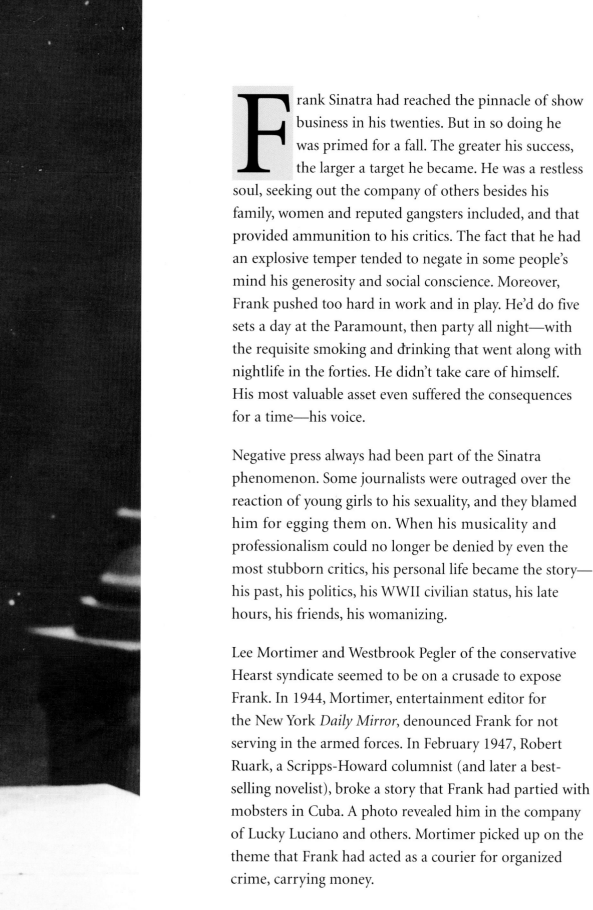

Frank Sinatra had reached the pinnacle of show business in his twenties. But in so doing he was primed for a fall. The greater his success, the larger a target he became. He was a restless soul, seeking out the company of others besides his family, women and reputed gangsters included, and that provided ammunition to his critics. The fact that he had an explosive temper tended to negate in some people's mind his generosity and social conscience. Moreover, Frank pushed too hard in work and in play. He'd do five sets a day at the Paramount, then party all night—with the requisite smoking and drinking that went along with nightlife in the forties. He didn't take care of himself. His most valuable asset even suffered the consequences for a time—his voice.

Negative press always had been part of the Sinatra phenomenon. Some journalists were outraged over the reaction of young girls to his sexuality, and they blamed him for egging them on. When his musicality and professionalism could no longer be denied by even the most stubborn critics, his personal life became the story—his past, his politics, his WWII civilian status, his late hours, his friends, his womanizing.

Lee Mortimer and Westbrook Pegler of the conservative Hearst syndicate seemed to be on a crusade to expose Frank. In 1944, Mortimer, entertainment editor for the New York *Daily Mirror*, denounced Frank for not serving in the armed forces. In February 1947, Robert Ruark, a Scripps-Howard columnist (and later a best-selling novelist), broke a story that Frank had partied with mobsters in Cuba. A photo revealed him in the company of Lucky Luciano and others. Mortimer picked up on the theme that Frank had acted as a courier for organized crime, carrying money.

On April 8, 1947, Frank punched Mortimer at Ciro's, a West Hollywood nightspot. The Hearst papers covered the incident in detail and repeated accusations of Frank's ties to the mob. Frank said he decked Mortimer because the columnist called him a "dago son of a bitch." Frank later had to pay Mortimer $9,000 and make a public apology.

In September 1947, Pegler wrote about the 1938-39 Toni Francke story without providing all the facts, in particular that the charges had been dismissed. He too attempted to link Frank to organized crime.

In the spring of 1949, gossip columnists such as Sheila Graham, Hedda Hopper, and Louella Parsons entertained their readers with reports of Frank's extramarital affairs. Frank didn't miss an opportunity to lash out at them, and soon his hostility toward many members of the press made him even more enemies. Many of them thought Sinatra's confidence had become arrogance, especially since the press has helped make him big. The Hollywood Women's Press Club voted Frank the "Least Cooperative Star" in 1946. He angered most of Hollywood when he said, "Pictures stink and most of the people in them do too," and his frequent statements that he was going to make pictures his way didn't help the situation. Although *Anchors Aweigh* had been a big hit in 1945, his next several films were failures.

This was also the heyday of Senator Joseph McCarthy and his House Un-American Activities Committee, and their accusations of Communist doings in the United States. Because of his support for civil rights, Frank was investigated by McCarthy's California supporters around the same time for possible Communist beliefs.

The final blow, fittingly, involved a woman. Accounts of Frank's affair with green-eyed Hollywood beauty Ava Gardner broke in late 1949. Nancy's filing for a legal separation in February 1950 was the climax of the story. Though Nancy had looked the other way for almost a decade while Frank carried on with other women, the public scrutiny this time was too much. Frank the cad … Ava the homewrecker … the moral temper of the times was strict, and the two were condemned for their public romance. And it made good copy and sold a lot of newspapers. His public image deteriorated even further. The boy next door, to many, had become the back door man.

"Being an eighteen-karat manic depressive and having lived a life of violent emotional contradictions, I have an overactive capacity for sadness as well as elation."

–Frank Sinatra

Previous page: Television's *The Frank Sinatra Show* (1959).

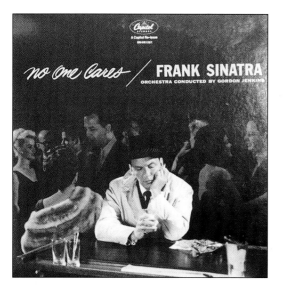

Meanwhile, Sinatra's popularity cooled toward the end of the decade. His records weren't selling and his movies weren't filling theaters. Johnnie Ray was the new teen heartthrob, and another Frankie, Frankie Laine, was also selling millions of records. No Sinatra records topped the charts in 1949; in May of that year, Frank was dropped from *Your Hit Parade*. His movie career was on the slide too. Frank originally was to receive top billing in promotion of *On the Town*; by the time the popular musical was released in December 1949, MGM decided to feature Gene Kelly instead. In April 1950, MGM canceled Frank's contract because of his declining box office draw and the negative image his breakup with Nancy had engendered. That also was the month that Frank's voice failed for the first time in concert, at the Copacabana in New York City, due to vocal-cord hemorrhaging. He had to slow down and take care of himself for a time before singing again. But a croak in his voice would persist.

Frank continued to work throughout his down period. In May 1950, he had made his television debut on *Bob Hope's Star Spangled Review*; the following October, *The Frank Sinatra Show*, a CBS television variety series, began a two-year run. But ratings were moderate.

Frank and Ava were married in November 1951. To some fans, the marriage seemed a glamorous union of two heavenly bodies; to others, it was a betrayal.

In June 1952, Frank's talent agency, MCA, let him go. That September, Frank made his last recording for Columbia Records, who had terminated their contract with him. Mitch Miller, the company's new A&R director following Manie Sachs, had tried to modernize Sinatra's sound without success. Frank's slow, heartfelt ballads weren't selling, so he even tried a few unsuccessful gimmick songs such as "Mama Will Bark," a novelty record with a one-name dumb blonde act named Dagmar and a barking dog. The times were changing, but Sinatra couldn't keep up with them.

With the downturn in his career, Frank began having financial problems. Though he'd been making millions in the mid-forties, living the high life had been costly and so was his divorce. Without a movie company, record company, or talent agency, he was reduced to borrowing from Ava. She helped him out financially and professionally as well. With her own career flourishing, she used her influence to get his back on track. But the storminess of their relationship put added stress on Frank.

In any case, by late 1952, as he was turning thirty-seven, Frank Sinatra seemed a stressed-out, washed-out has-been.

"My singing went downhill and I went downhill with it, or vice versa... It happened because I paid no attention to how I was singing. Instead, I wanted to sit back and enjoy my success and sign autographs and bank the heavy cash... The only guy who can hurt you is yourself."

—Frank Sinatra

Ava Gardner was successful, beautiful, voluptuous, elegant, sultry, naughty—larger than life, it seemed. The sharecropper's daughter with the thick Southern accent (before her studio insisted she take diction lessons) had come from rural North Carolina to make it in Hollywood, starting out as a model before landing small roles. Her incandescent onscreen performance in her first starring role, in *The Killers* (1946), along with her fiery temper, impetuosity, and offscreen outspokenness, made her a national obsession in the forties and fifties, much as Frank Sinatra was. Like Frank, she was a heavy drinker and night owl. And they were both moody, possessive, and temperamental. It made perfect sense that they would find each other.

The two celebrities met for the first time in April 1945 at a Hollywood nightclub, a year after Frank had moved west. Ava had divorced actor Mickey Rooney two years before after a marriage of less than a year. Frank began flirting right away as he would whenever they ran into each other over the next few years on RKO and MGM sets. She originally told friends she found Frank conceited, arrogant, and overpowering (and she knew he had a wife and children). But the tension between these two strong-willed people only seemed to draw them together. Frank continued the flirtation with the green-eyed Southern beauty at every opportunity. He often stayed over at his songwriter friend Sammy Cahn's apartment to drink and play cards, rather than go home to Toluca Lake. Ava lived across the street and he and his buddies would shout to her from Cahn's balcony. She didn't answer.

In early 1948, Frank asked Ava out for dinner and drinks. This time she accepted his advances. She had been married again since meeting Frank—to bandleader Artie Shaw—but only for ten months. Her failed marriages and his pursuit of her made his marital status seem less important this time around. The first Frank and Ava date ended in some necking in a friend's apartment but nothing more.

Bewitched

Ava

"Bewitched, bothered and bewildered am I . . ."

Frank and Ava met at a party in Palm Springs in February 1949 and both acted somewhat sheepish about what had happened the year before. But now their relationship felt inevitable. They began seeing each other steadily, usually at friends' houses. But in December 1949, the public began to take notice. They were spotted together at the premiere of *Gentlemen Prefer Blondes* in New York and later at the Hampshire House Hotel, where Frank's friend, Manie Sachs of Columbia Records, had a suite. Negative publicity resulted despite denials of a relationship. In his last stand on behalf of Frank's image, press agent George Evans, while denying all rumors publicly, advised Frank privately against involvement with Ava. (Evans died of a heart attack the following January.) On January 28, 1950, Ava joined Frank in Houston, where he was performing for the opening of the Shamrock Hotel. This time, a photographer snapped pictures of them together despite Frank's angry protestations.

Long-suffering Nancy Sinatra felt the time had come to let go. On February 14—Valentine's Day—she petitioned for a legal separation. Frank and Ava's romance was the biggest story going, and the press hounded them. That May, it was reported that Frank canceled a singing engagement in Chicago to fly to Spain where Ava was filming *Pandora and the Flying Dutchman* because of competition from Mario Cabre, a bullfighter appearing in the movie. Sinatra had been let go by MGM in April, the same month his throat had hemorrhaged.

Frank obtained a Nevada divorce from Nancy on November 1, 1951. He and Ava were married less than a week later on November 7 at the home of Lester Sachs, Manie's brother, in suburban Philadelphia. Arranger Axel Stordahl was the best man.

The marriage, despite Frank and Ava's intense love for each other, was in trouble from the outset. Both Frank and Ava were mercurial and insanely jealous, and fights often erupted. The fact that Frank's career was in decline while Ava's was peaking put added pressures on them. Her time away from him when filming inevitably led to problems between them, such as her departure for Kenya for the filming of *The Snows of Kilimanjaro* in early 1952, and Ava had to juggle her shooting schedule to appease him. Meanwhile, she threw jealous fits if Frank were attentive to other women.

"This love I feel for her [Ava Gardner], it's sapping me of everything I got. I got no energy left for anything. What is this spell she has me under?"

–Frank Sinatra

Above: At the Hollywood premiere of *Showboat* (1951).

Left, above, and overleaf: The wedding day, November 7, 1951.

Above: At the New York premiere of
The Snows of Kilamanjaro (1952).

Previous spread: First stop on the honeymoon
was Miami Beach.

In 1952, Ava had two abortions (in England, where it was legal), unwilling to take on the responsibility of a child. Frank knew nothing of the first pregnancy until later. At the time of her second pregnancy, he argued in favor of keeping the child, but Ava had made up her mind against it.

Ava did what she could to help Frank's career back on track. She lobbied on his behalf with the wife of Harry Cohn, producer of *From Here to Eternity*. Landing the role of Maggio rallied Frank's career in 1953, but it didn't save his second marriage.

Their separation was announced in October 1953. Several reconciliations were attempted. That December, Ava flew from Rome, where she was filming *The Barefoot Contessa*, to Madrid to spend Christmas with another bullfighter, Luis Dominguin. Frank joined her there in the hope of saving the marriage, then went to Italy with her. But they couldn't come to terms. Frank returned alone to his Wilshire Boulevard apartment in Los Angeles.

Neither Frank nor Ava filed for divorce for several years; they remained officially married until July 5, 1957. And neither lost the flame for the other. At one point Frank tore up her picture in a fit of anger, but he pasted it back together and kept it up on his dressing room wall. Ava would claim years later that she never loved another man the way she loved Frank. And more than any other relationship, Frank's failed love for Ava was the impetus for many of his greatest recordings. "It was Ava who taught him how to sing a torch song," said arranger Nelson Riddle, who would team with Sinatra for his greatest recordings. "That's how he learned. She was the greatest love of his life, and he lost her."

The Best Is Yet to Come

The Comeback

*"Still it's a real good bet,
the best is yet to come . . ."*

Frank Sinatra was a driven man, a fighter. His hard work and talent had paid off for him in the past. In his darkest hour, in 1952, he felt he needed just one break, just one lucky throw of the dice, to get his career back on track. He was right.

In James Jones's bestselling novel *From Here to Eternity* (1951) the character Private Angelo Maggio, stationed in Pearl Harbor, is an Italian-American from a poor neighborhood with a big heart but a bad temper. In Maggio, Frank saw a lot of himself. On learning that the book was being made into a movie, Frank began a full-bore effort to land the role. He contacted the producer, Buddy Adler, as well as the head of Columbia Pictures, Harry Cohn, offering to do the role for a mere $8,000 (his former price had been $150,000 per picture). Ava Gardner spoke to Cohn's wife, Joan, about Frank being a true-to-life Maggio. Frank's new agency, the William Morris Agency, also lobbied the resistant Cohn on his behalf.

In December 1952, Frank flew to Kenya to be with Ava Gardner while she filmed *Mogambo*. Five days after his arrival there, he was summoned back to the U.S. for a screen test. Then it was down to just two contenders: Sinatra and highly regarded stage actor Eli Wallach. Finally, it was announced: the skinny Italian-American would play the skinny Italian-American. Rumors of *Godfather*-style mob threats were rampant, but all parties involved agree that it came down to one simple fact: Sinatra was perfect for the part.

Landing the role helped re-energize Frank. Filming began in April, and the daily rushes were so good that the film was fast-tracked for release on August 17, 1953. It was a huge success, the most popular movie in Columbia's history, and enthusiastic critics took notice of Sinatra's powerful performance. The fact that the intense but likable Maggio was killed in a fight with a bully captivated audiences, making the real-life Frank more human to them.

The following March, at the Academy Awards, Frank received an Oscar for Best Supporting Actor. Little Nancy and Frank Jr. were there with him to celebrate his triumph. His success changed everything. Meaty film roles were offered to him. In 1956, Frank would be nominated for an Oscar as Best Actor for his performance as a heroin addict in *The Man with the Golden Arm* (1955).

Frank's recording career came back to life in 1953 too. Since Columbia had dropped him, he had been crisscrossing the country performing fresh new arrangements of the classic American songbook, playing at small clubs and singing his voice back into shape. In April, Frank signed with the fledgling Capitol Records after another former Tommy Dorsey singer, Jo Stafford, told the label how good he sounded. After one session with longtime friend and arranger Axel Stordahl that broke little new ground, Frank was teamed with music arranger (and former Tommy Dorsey trombonist) Nelson Riddle on April 30. The first song recorded was "I've Got the World on a String," and the rest was history. It was the beginning of a brilliant collaboration, during which what is considered the classic "Sinatra sound" took shape. Riddle's jazz-influenced, swinging arrangements, bolstered by uptempo beats and driving horns and reeds, contrasted with Stordahl's Germanic strings and ponderous ballads. A listener could snap his fingers to Frank's lively new sound, and music lovers responded instantly. Within months a string of hits began; it seemed every single released—and there were dozens during the next decade—reached the top five on the *Billboard* charts. The long-playing record had recently arrived on the scene, and Frank's first LPs with Capitol, *Songs for Young Lovers* and *Swing Easy,* also were received with acclaim. They were concept albums, considered the first, a progression of songs telling a story. Other high-quality albums resulting from the Sinatra-Riddle collabortion followed: The saloon-song filled *In the Wee Small Hours* in 1955; *Songs for Swingin' Lovers!* in 1956; *A Swingin' Affair* in 1957; and *Only the Lonely* in 1958. From 1957 to 1966, Sinatra delivered twenty Top Ten albums. (In a fans' poll of the favorite Sinatra song of all time, "I've Got You Under My Skin" from *Songs for Swingin' Lovers!* won.)

"Luck is only important insofar as getting the chance to sell yourself at the right moment. After that, you've got to have talent and know how to use it. It would be more accurate to call what happened to my career the rise and fall and rise again."

—Frank Sinatra

Right: Sinatra, nightclub owner Monte Proser, and Nat "King" Cole at New York's La Vie en Rose, 1952.

On August 29, 1955, Frank made the cover of *Time* magazine; the article stated that he was on the verge of being the "greatest all-around entertainer in show business." At the end of 1956, he was named among the Top Ten Money-Making Stars in the Motion Picture Herald poll. On October 18, 1957, *The Frank Sinatra Show* debuted with ABC-TV. Frank was given carte-blanche to shape this series of twenty-one one-hour musical variety shows and ten half-hour dramas. In 1959, he won a Grammy for Album of the Year, *Come Dance with Me*, as well as for Best Solo Vocal Performance, "Come Dance with Me."

Frank, now recognized as the greatest song stylist of the twentieth century, sold out concert engagements; his records topped the charts; he received good notices for his acting; he was all over the media; and he was winning awards. He was, simply, the most powerful individual in show business.

He also was redefining personal behavior—his and his friends' late night, live-life-to-the-fullest antics—as well as personal style: snap-brim hat, trench coat flung over the shoulder, always smartly dressed. Once again in life, he was on a winning streak. He would continue to have personal problems and he would continue to make headlines with his rash behavior, but he never again would lose his professional stature.

"I started out the decade as 'the man least likely' and closed it out as a grateful human being, given a second shot at life."

–Frank Sinatra

Frank was able to translate his charismatic onstage personality to his screen performances. The subtlety of his expressions—his gaze, his smile—worked well for the camera. His early roles were minuscule and mostly involved singing, but they helped him learn to be comfortable in front of a camera. And Frank's understated onscreen style has improved with age—there are few false moves or overdone histrionics in his almost sixty screen performances.

At age nineteen, Frank sang in two one-reel shorts when under contract with *Major Bowes and His Original Amateur Hour*, as a waiter in *The Night Club* and a member of a blackface singing troupe in *The Big Minstrel Act*. Frank reportedly never saw either one. In 1941, Frank appeared in *Las Vegas Nights* and *Ship Ahoy*, singing with Tommy Dorsey's band. In Frank's first feature film without the Dorsey band, Columbia Pictures' *Reveille with Beverly* (1943), he sings one song, "Night and Day."

In September 1943, Frank signed with RKO Pictures. *Higher and Higher* was released three months later. Frank, in his first speaking role, plays himself and sings five songs. In *Step Lively* (1944), Frank gives and takes his first screen kiss; the actress was Gloria DeHaven. Frank plays a priest in *The Miracle of the Bells* (1946), co-starring Fred MacMurray and Lee J. Cobb; he sings only one song. In *Double Dynamite* (1951), Frank performs a comedic role alongside Groucho Marx and Jane Russell, again singing only one song.

In February 1944, Frank signed a five-year contract with MGM Pictures for $1.5 million. In the most memorable of his music-oriented MGM movies—*Anchors Aweigh* (1945), *Take Me Out to the Ballgame* (1949), and *On the Town* (1949)—Frank was paired with Gene Kelly, who helped teach Frank how to dance beginning in *Anchors Aweigh*. The cream of the crop, though, is *On the Town*, the first musical to be shot on location in New York City. A stellar cast and lively Bernstein score made it one of MGM's most enjoyable musicals. Other early MGM films with Frank playing lead roles included *It Happened in Brooklyn* (1947) with Jimmy Durante and Peter Lawford (who later became a member of the Rat Pack); and *The Kissing Bandit* (1948), in which Frank again plays a priest.

From Here
to Eternity

The Actor

"A love so true it would never die . . ."

None of his acting roles through the forties were nominated for an Oscar, but Sinatra did receive a special Academy Award—not as an actor, but for social commitment because of his involvement in RKO's *The House I Live In* (1945). In this ten-minute short, Frank lectures a group of boys on racial and religious tolerance and sings two songs, including the title song.

In Universal International's *Meet Danny Wilson* (1951), Frank plays a crooner up against a racketeering nightclub owner played by Raymond Burr. Frank sings nine songs, including "That Old Black Magic" and "All of Me."

So far, so good—but nothing extraordinary. The movie that established Frank's career as a dramatic actor was Columbia Pictures' *From Here to Eternity* (1953), based on the novel by James Jones and directed by Fred Zinnemann. The powerhouse cast included Burt Lancaster, Montgomery Clift, Deborah Kerr, Donna Reed, and Ernest Borgnine. Frank threw himself into the project, even undergoing several hours of military training a day to prepare for his role as Private Angelo Maggio. The movie won an Oscar for Best Picture plus seven others, including Frank for Best Supporting Actor and Donna Reed for Best Supporting Actress. Frank also won a Golden Globe for Best Supporting Actor.

Suddenly the actor who a few years before was without a movie, record, TV, or radio contract was again on top of the entertainment world. Frank's acting career was firmly established. In the years to come, he appeared in many movies—in starring roles and in guest appearances as well. For a good part of the fifties, he was the hottest commodity in Hollywood. Now he could pick and choose his roles, and he threw himself into acting with a string of interesting roles.

In United Artists' *Suddenly* (1954), Frank gives a powerful performance as a heavy, a gunman hired to assassinate the President. In Warner Brothers' *Young at Heart* (1954), Frank appears with Doris Day and sings five songs, among them the title song. In United Artists' medical melodrama *Not as a Stranger* (1955), Frank acts alongside Robert Mitchum and Olivia de Havilland. In MGM's *The Tender Trap* (1955), Frank shares the spotlight with Debbie Reynolds and again sings the title song.

Previous page: *The Naked Runner* (1967).

Right: Montgomery Clift, Burt Lancaster, and Sinatra on the set of *From Here to Eternity* (1953).

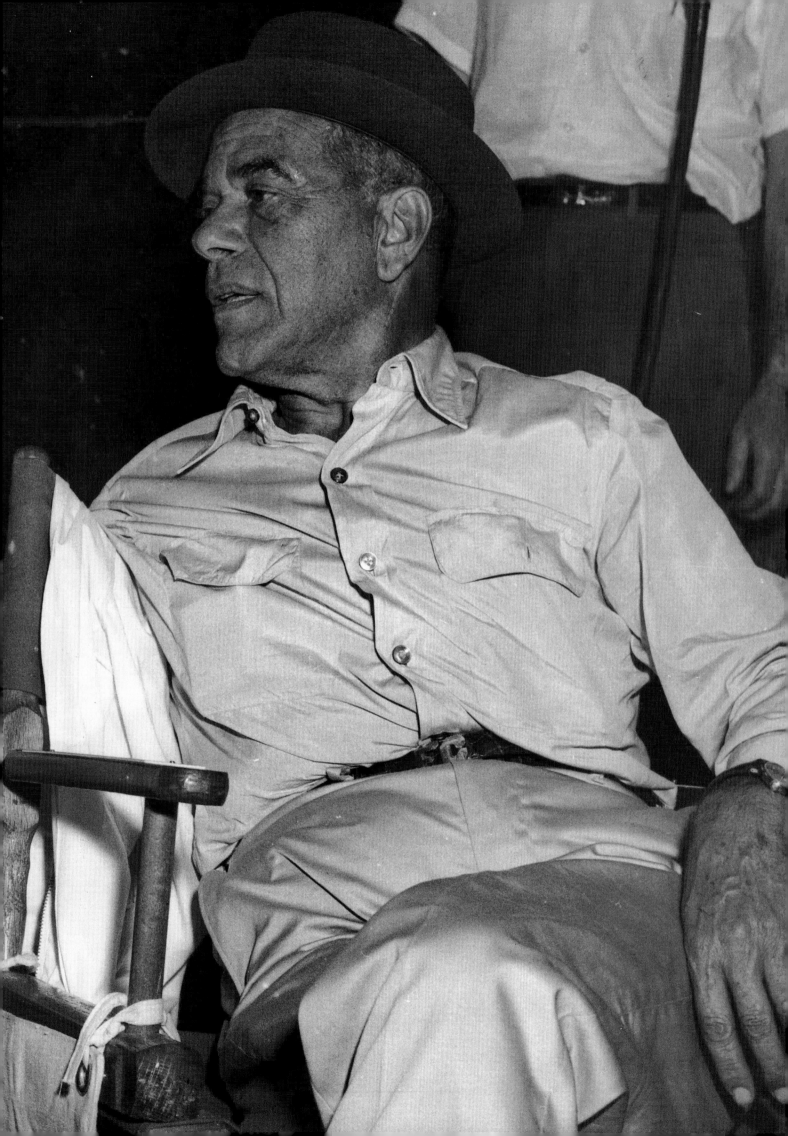

MGM's *Guys and Dolls* (1955) was a successful movie version of the stage musical. Frank plays the role of gangster Nathan Detroit opposite Marlon Brando as Sky Masterson. Interestingly, Frank landed the non-singing role; Brando, the non-singer, got to sing in the role Frank coveted—Frank Loesser's score was one of the finest ever written. Though Sinatra thought Brando's Method acting was a lot of hooey and called him "Mumbles," the two got along well during filming.

In United Artists' *The Man with the Golden Arm* (1955), directed by Otto Preminger, Frank delivered what he considered his best performance. He acted opposite Kim Novak as Frankie Machine, a drummer, card shark, and heroin addict. Frank's cold-turkey withdrawal scene probably contains the best acting he ever did. He was nominated for Best Actor for this role, although he didn't win.

Sinatra received his first credit as a producer for United Artists' *Johnny Concho* (1956), a minor western with Frank as the title character. In MGM's *High Society* (1956), Frank was teamed up with his early idol, Bing Crosby, and their duet, "Well, Did You Evah?," is the highlight of the film. Grace Kelly is the object of both their desires in the adaptation of *The Philadelphia Story*. Cole Porter wrote the fine musical score.

In the United Artists drama *The Pride and the Passion* (1957), Frank plays a Spanish peasant opposite Sophia Loren. Though miscast, he gave a good account of himself. Paramount's *The Joker is Wild* (1957) is a biographical account of entertainer Joe E. Lewis; Frank is excellent as his good friend Lewis, a singer whose throat was sliced by mobsters but who managed a comeback as a comedian. One of four songs Frank sings, "All the Way," won an Academy Award for best song.

In Columbia Pictures' *Pal Joey* (1957), a screen version of the Rodgers and Hart musical, Frank found a role perfect for both his singing and his personality—as the caddish singer Joey Evans, caught between two women, played by Rita Hayworth and Kim Novak. "The Lady Is a Tramp," sung to Hayworth, was the highlight here.

Previous spread: Sinatra and director Frank Capra on the set of *A Hole in the Head* (1959).

Left: Bing Crosby, Grace Kelly, and Sinatra in a publicity pose for *High Society* (1956).

United Artists' *Kings Go Forth* (1958), a World War II story, pairs Frank with Natalie Wood and Tony Curtis. In MGM's *Some Came Running* (1958), a postwar story based on a novel by James Jones and directed by Vincente Minnelli, Frank acts alongside Shirley MacLaine and Dean Martin, who would become his most frequent co-star. The movie contained another excellent Sinatra performance. Frank Capra produced and directed United Artists' *A Hole in the Head* (1959), co-starring Edward G. Robinson. Sinatra's duet with young Eddie Hodges, "High Hopes," went on to win an Oscar as Best Song.

In MGM's *Never So Few* (1959), Frank appears in another World War II story, this time opposite Gina Lollobrigida. The cast includes Peter Lawford, Charles Bronson, and Steve McQueen (who was more than Frank's match in location clowning), and Charles Bronson. Frank again is teamed with Shirley MacLaine and again sings songs by Cole Porter in 20th Century-Fox's *Can-Can* (1960), Frank's final musical.

The comedy-drama *Ocean's Eleven* (1960), from Warner Bros. in association with Frank's Dorchester production company, tells the story of a Las Vegas casino heist and brings together the inner circle of Frank's show-business friends, who became known as the "Rat Pack"—Frank, Dean Martin, Sammy Davis Jr., Peter Lawford, and Joey Bishop. Angie Dickinson, who was a "token broad" of the Rat Pack, also appears in the film. It's the best of the full-scale Rat Pack movies, and an enjoyable caper film.

Columbia Picture's *The Devil at Four O'Clock* (1961) tells the story of a volcano about to erupt on a South Pacific island. Frank plays a convict with a big heart to Spencer Tracy's heroic priest. United Artists' *Sergeants 3* (1962), a western, produced by Frank, is another Rat Pack movie—this one a remake of *Gunga Din* set in the American West.

United Artists' *The Manchurian Candidate* (1962) was perhaps Frank's last great role in a truly excellent film. In this powerful Cold War psychodrama directed by John Frankenheimer, Frank stars with Laurence Harvey and Janet Leigh. Because there were similarities in the movie to the the real-life assassination of President Kennedy, his good friend, Frank withdrew it from circulation for twenty-five years (and did the same with *Suddenly*, for similar reasons).

Left: At the 35th Annual Academy Awards presentation.

"He (Gene Kelly) taught me everything I know. He's one of the reasons I became a star. He's always been one of my great friends."

–Frank Sinatra

Left: Sinatra and Gene Kelly in a scene from
Anchors Aweigh (1945).

Above: Sinatra, Bing Crosby, and Dean Martin record a song from
Guys and Dolls in 1963 for an album in a series of Broadway musicals
with new arrangements and singers.

Left: With Jane Powell on a forties movie set.

Above: With Edward Wallerstein, the president of Columbia Records, and Abe Lastfogle, the president of the William Morris Agency.

Frank's performance is one of his most passionate and moving, along with *From Here to Eternity* and *The Man with the Golden Arm.*

Frank sings the title song of Paramount's drama *Come Blow Your Horn* (1963), co-starring Lee J. Cobb, Tony Bill, Jill St. John, and Dean Martin. Warner Bros.' *4 for Texas* (1963) brought Frank and Dean Martin together again, as did Warner Bros.' *Robin and the 7 Hoods* (1964). Sammy Davis Jr., Bing Crosby, Edward G. Robinson, and Peter Falk also appear in *Robin and the 7 Hoods*, produced by Frank.

Sinatra made his directorial debut in and produced Warner Bros.' *None But the Brave* (1965), an anti-war story set on a South Pacific island during World War II. 20th Century-Fox's *Von Ryan's Express* (1965) is another World War II movie, with Frank playing Colonel Joseph L. Ryan, leader of a group of POWs who seize a Nazi train. Sinatra is surprisingly effective in a part that was originally written as a tall, strapping, blond Irish-American. In Warner Bros.' *Marriage on the Rocks* (1965), with Dean Martin and Deborah Kerr, Frank's daughter Nancy makes an appearance.

In Paramount's *Assault on a Queen* (1966), Frank plays an ex-submarine officer involved in an attempt to hijack the *Queen Mary*. Warner Bros.' *The Naked Runner* (1967) is a Cold War spy thriller, with Frank playing a businessman sucked into an assassination plot. In his next three movies— 20th Century-Fox's *Tony Rome* (1967), *The Detective* (1968), and *Lady in Cement* (1968)—Sinatra makes convincing turns as detectives; his three co-stars respectively were Jill St. John, Lee Remick, and Raquel Welch. *The Detective* was the best of the trio. In MGM's western comedy *Dirty Dingus Magee* (1970), Frank plays the title character, a thieving rascal in 1880s New Mexico; the results weren't memorable.

Frank plays a deputy police inspector in Columbia's made-for-television movie *Contract on Cherry Street* (1977). Filmways' urban crime drama, *The First Deadly Sin* (1980), was Frank's last lead role, again as a detective, with Faye Dunaway as his wife. He went out on a high note; his final performance was a strong one, and the movie his best since *The Detective* twelve years earlier.

Above: Sinatra in a scene from *Higher and Higher* (1944).

Right: Rosemary Clooney, Sinatra, and Bing Crosby.

"He (Bing Crosby) was the father of my career,
the idol of my youth—and the dear,
dear friend of my maturity."

–Frank Sinatra

Debbie Reynolds outlines for David Wayne, Celeste Holm and Frank Sinatra her complete plan for a happy marriage.

M·G·M's CinemaScope "THE TENDER TRAP" in Color

Copyright 1955 Loew's Incorporated   COUNTRY OF ORIGIN U. S. A.   4   Property of National Screen Service Corp. Licensed for display only in connection with the exhibition of this picture at your theatre. Must be returned immediately thereafter.   55-456

An adult look at a police detective.

FRANK SINATRA
THE DETECTIVE

RODERICK THORP'S GIANT NOVEL COMES ON LIKE A POWERHOUSE!

LEE REMICK   RALPH MEEKER JACK KLUGMAN LLOYD BOCHNER WILLIAM WINDOM TONY MUSANTE AL FREEMAN JR. ROBERT DUVALL · JACQUELINE BISSET

It's kind of a western.
He's sort of a cowboy.

SINATRA IS
DIRTY DINGUS MAGEE

METRO-GOLDWYN-MAYER Presents A BURT KENNEDY PRODUCTION Starring
FRANK SINATRA and GEORGE KENNEDY in "DIRTY DINGUS MAGEE"
WITH ANNE JACKSON co-starring MICHELE CAREY · LOIS NETTLETON · JACK ELAM
Screenplay by TOM WALDMAN & FRANK WALDMAN and JOSEPH HELLER Based on "The Ballad of Dingus Magee" by DAVID MARKSON
Produced and Directed By BURT KENNEDY PANAVISION METROCOLOR   GP   MGM

Dave was back and the whole town knew that trouble—and women—were close behind!

From the bold, new novel by the author of "From Here To Eternity"

FRANK SINATRA
DEAN MARTIN
SHIRLEY MacLAINE

M·G·M presents A SOL C. SIEGEL PRODUCTION

..."SOME CAME RUNNING"

MARTHA HYER   ARTHUR KENNEDY
NANCY GATES   LEORA DANA

Screen Play by JOHN PATRICK and ARTHUR SHEEKMAN · Based on the Novel by JAMES JONES · in CinemaScope and METROCOLOR · Directed by VINCENTE MINNELLI

Frank also made a number of cameo movie appearances, often as himself, and also appeared in a number of documentaries. In MGM's films on the company's golden age of musicals, *That's Entertainment* (1974) and *That's Entertainment, Part II* (1976), Frank acts as co-host—and appears in a few of the many memorable sequences included.

Over the years, Sinatra appeared on numerous television variety shows as a host or as a guest. His appearances revolved around his singing, but he performed numerous skits as well. In 1955, he played a dramatic role as the Stage Manager and sang songs in an NBC television version of Thornton Wilder's play *Our Town*. One of his songs, "Love and Marriage" by Sammy Cahn and Jimmy Van Heusen, won an Emmy.

Frank was an intuitive actor who didn't like doing more than one or two takes, especially later in his career. He firmly believed that his best performance would be on the first take, before the freshness was hammered out of him by repeated line deliveries. And his understated, low-key style has worn well. It's the rare Sinatra role that isn't more than watchable, and a few of his performances rank with the best onscreen jobs of acting in film history.

Left: *Von Ryan's Express* (1965).

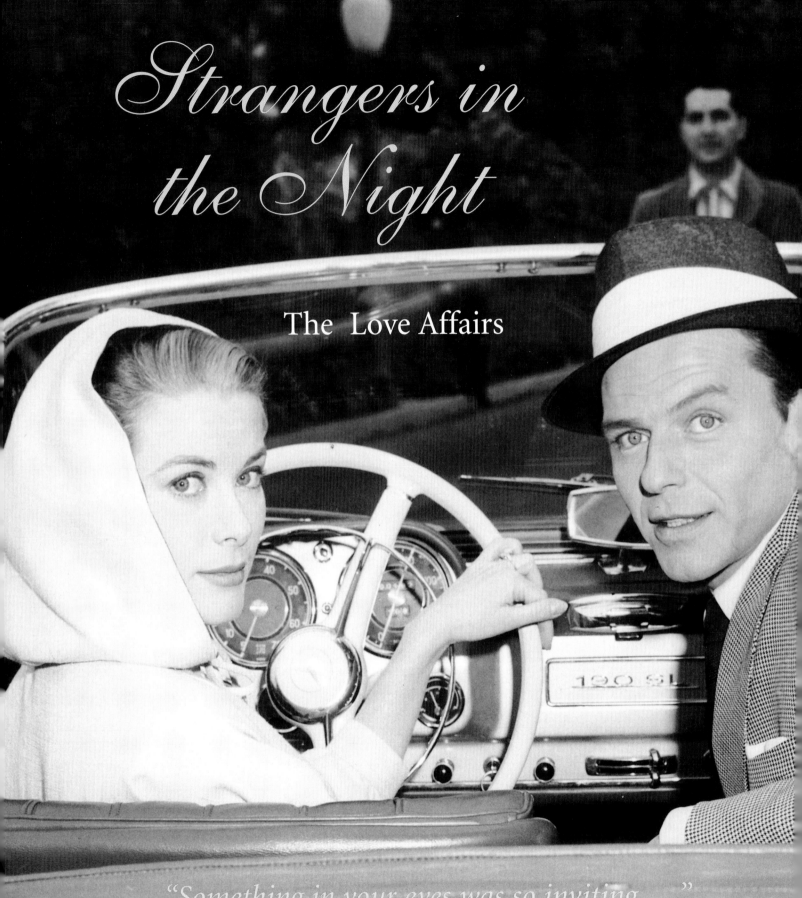

Strangers in the Night

The Love Affairs

"Something in your eyes was so inviting . . ."

Frank Sinatra was a man who loved women—and as a star, he was loved and adored in return. But Frank, as of the age twenty-three, was married to the girl next door. Nancy Barbato Sinatra also became the mother of his children. When Frank hit it big and became distanced from his wife, he had to be discreet in his affairs. Some of them with fellow celebrities, in particular Marilyn Maxwell and Lana Turner, received press attention, but he could dismiss them as rumors. When his publicly revealed affair with Ava Gardner could no longer be denied, it caused the breakup of his first marriage. His second marriage, to Ava, was stormy and short-lived. Following his 1957 divorce from her (and during their earlier separation), Sinatra dated many women—budding starlets, successful actresses, and society women. The extent of most of his relationships cannot be documented. But, at the least, each was an intense flirtation. And Frank was a master at it. He was famous for his lavish attention to women—the intensity of his gaze ("the blue-eyed ray," as songwriter Sammy Cahn called it), the cleverness of his come-ons, and the expansiveness of his gifts. The sheer overwhelming attention he concentrated on a woman proved irresistible time and again.

The list of celebrities linked with Frank over the years goes on and on: Lauren Bacall, Lady Adele Beatty, Jacqueline Bisset, Linda Christian, Peggy Connolly, Joan Crawford, Angie Dickinson, Marlene Dietrich, Patty Duke, Anita Ekberg, Betty Furness, Eva and Zsa Zsa Gabor, Judy Garland, Grace Kelly, Hope Lange, Peggy Lipton, Gina Lollobrigida, Sophia Loren, Carol Lynley, Shirley MacLaine, Marilyn Monroe, Lois Nettleton, Kim Novak, Jacqueline Kennedy Onassis, Victoria Principal, Dorothy Provine, Juliet Prowse, Nancy (Davis) Reagan, Lee Remick, Debbie Reynolds, Jill St. John, Elizabeth Taylor, Gloria Vanderbilt, Tuesday Weld, Natalie Wood. Many of these women appeared in movies with Frank. Even when the cameras stopped rolling, he apparently kept playing the scene with them.

Sinatra, mostly for his children's sake, guarded his privacy about his affairs. If a woman friend betrayed this trust, he was liable to end the relationship. In 1957, an actress by the name of Shirley Van Dyke mentioned his name in a suicide note when taking an overdose of pills (she recovered). Although he was supportive of her career beforehand, he had nothing to do with her afterwards. Frank also would end a relationship on the spot if crossed or insulted. When Edith Goetz, daughter of Louis B. Mayer (of MGM) and widow of producer William Goetz, reportedly joked that Frank was "nothing but a hoodlum," he refused to see her again.

Marilyn Monroe actually lived in Frank's apartment for a time in 1954, when he was still lovesick over Ava, and she over her former husband, baseball great Joe DiMaggio. Their relationship began as platonic, with Frank assuming the role of a protector, but they eventually became intimate. Frank claimed he loved her but never was in love with her. That relationship put an end to a close friendship with DiMaggio, who never stopped carrying a torch for Monroe.

Two of Frank's longest-lasting relationships were with Lauren Bacall ("Betty" to friends, since her real name was Betty Persky) following her husband Humphrey Bogart's death in January 1957, and with Juliet Prowse, a South African dancer he met on the set of *Can-Can* in 1959. The press tracked these stories relentlessly, embellishing them at times and even playing a part in their outcome.

Sinatra was known for being helpful to women at trying times in their lives. He had a knack for lending a shoulder to grief-stricken widows. He helped Bacall cope with Bogart's nearly year-long bout with cancer. He himself was at a difficult time in life due to his breakup with Ava; the two comforted each other. Following Bogart's death in January 1957, Frank and Bacall's friendship evolved into a solid relationship. Frank proposed to her in March 1958. When columnist Louella Parsons wrote about their engagement, Frank blamed Bacall for revealing it (although she claimed in her autobiography that a mutual friend had done so, show biz agent Irving "Swifty" Lazar) and called off the marriage. The two reportedly didn't speak for six years.

Previous page: Sinatra and Grace Kelly in *High Society* (1956).

Right: Sinatra with Jacqueline Onassis, 1975.

"*Women, I don't know what the hell to make of them, do you?*"

–Frank Sinatra

"The trouble with Sinatra is that he thinks heaven is a place where there are all broads and no newspapermen. He doesn't know that he'd be better off if it were the other way around."

—Humphrey Bogart

Left: With Lauren Bacall, late fifties.

Above: *High Society* (1956).

"He (Sinatra) wasn't a womanizer—
he was womanized!
What a great position to be in."

–Tony Curtis

In the case of Juliet Prowse, an announcement came of their engagement in January 1963. Several months later, word came that the engagement was off. Some reports had it that it was all a ploy to further her career.

Frank, a hopeless romantic and at the same time a cynic about relationships based on his experiences, waffled on the issue of marriage for some years. That would change in 1966 when Frank once again tied the knot—with Mia Farrow.

I've Got the World on a String

Chairman of the Board

"Life's a wonderful thing . . .

By the 1960s, Frank Sinatra was a national institution. His name cropped up all over the media with regard to music, movies, business, politics, and gossip. The Voice was now the Chairman of the Board, the most powerful performer in show biz.

Musically, Frank was going strong—strong enough to risk founding his own record company. He wanted greater creative control of his projects, especially with regard to maintaining the "live" feel in recorded music, with minimal use of overdubbing and multiple tracks, practices that were becoming prevalent in the music business, and he wanted more equitable financial arrangements for the "talent." The record company he dubbed "Reprise" was the answer.

On December 19, 1960, Frank recorded his first cuts for Reprise, with jazz arranger Johnny Mandel; the first Reprise album, *Ring-a-Ding-Ding*, was released in February 1961. (Frank's contract with Capitol carried over two years; his final release with that label was *Sinatra Sings of Love and Things* in 1962.) A series of huge hit singles would follow, even as rock'n'roll was overwhelming the marketplace: "It Was a Very Good Year" in 1965, "Strangers in the Night" and "That's Life" in 1966, and "My Way" in 1969, all four considered Sinatra anthems. "Somethin' Stupid," recorded with his daughter Nancy in 1967, also was a big hit for Reprise.

As he had in 1959, Frank won a Grammy for Best Album of the Year (*September of My Years*) and Best Solo Vocal Performance ("It Was a Very Good Year") in 1965. The next year, he won a Grammy for Best Album of the Year (*Sinatra: A Man and his Music*) and Best Record of the Year ("Strangers in the Night"). Frank's music was honored in a unique way on July 20, 1969. On the Apollo 11 mission to the moon, the astronauts beamed back to Earth Frank's rendition of "Fly Me to the Moon." That song was a cut from *It Might As Well Be Swing*, an album he recorded with one of his musical idols, Count Basie; he would record two other albums with Basie and one with another major influence, Duke Ellington.

Previous page: Sinatra and Lee Iacocca.

Right: The 1965 NBC-TV special, *Frank Sinatra: A Man and His Music.*

"*He seemed now to be the embodiment of the fully emancipated male, perhaps the only one in America, the man who can do anything he wants, anything, can do it because he has the money, the energy, and no apparent guilt.*"

—*Gay Talese*

Frank meanwhile continued to perform for sold-out audiences worldwide as far afield as Australia. In the course of his benefit World Tour for Children in 1962, Frank performed in Hong Kong, Israel, Greece, Italy, England, France, and Monaco.

Frank, a potent box-office draw, had enormous power in the movie industry as well as the music business. He produced *Ocean's Eleven* (1960), as well as a number of other films. He also directed *None But the Brave* (1965). During this period, he also gave one of his most memorable performances in John Frankenheimer's *The Manchurian Candidate* (1963).

While dominating in music and movies, Frank kept his hand in television as well. On May 12, 1960, Frank hosted *The Frank Sinatra-Timex Special: Welcome Home Elvis* on ABC. The theme of the show involved showing Elvis what he had missed while in the Army in Germany. Each performed a number of songs. One of these was a duet in which they traded verses, Frank belting "Love Me Tender" and Elvis crooning "Witchcraft." The show's ratings went through the roof. In the ensuing years, Frank made guest appearances on a number of variety shows, among them shows hosted by Judy Garland, Dinah Shore, Bob Hope, Bing Crosby, and Ed Sullivan.

Meanwhile, Frank was expanding his business interests beyond music and movies. On August 15, 1961, along with partners Henry Sanicola and Sanford Waterman, Frank founded Park Lake Enterprises, Inc., opening Cal-Neva Lodge in Lake Tahoe, Nevada. This interest along with his share of the Sands Hotel in Las Vegas, which he had held since 1954, provided additional income through the end of 1963.

Frank's personal life continued to fascinate the public. During the sixties, the antics of Frank and his group of friends known as the "Rat Pack"—in particular Dean Martin, Sammy Davis Jr., Peter Lawford, and Joey Bishop—became a favorite subject of the media. And, as always, the love life of eligible bachelor Frank, such as his engagement to Juliet Prowse in 1962, and his engagement to and eventual marriage to Mia Farrow in 1966 (and their divorce in 1968), sold newspaper and magazines.

"I will always think of him (Sinatra) as the lovable land mine— something no sturdy American household should be without."

–Peter Lawford

Above: The May 1960 Frank Sinatra-Timex Special:
Welcome Home Elvis.

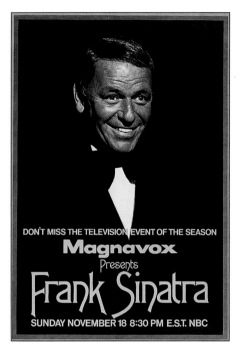

Frank's influence extended beyond popular culture. He actively campaigned on behalf of his friend John F. Kennedy in his successful run for the presidency, and he personally produced the inaugural ball in 1961. Frank subsequently visited with JFK at his Hyannisport vacation home, on his yacht, and on the presidential plane.

Yet during the sixties, Frank endured hardship as well, especially in late 1963. In September of that year, he was investigated by the Nevada Gaming Control Board and eventually forced to give up his license and sell out his shares in the Cal-Neva Lodge and the Sands Hotel. He was devastated by President Kennedy's assassination the following November. Only sixteen days later, another ordeal began for him—the kidnapping of his nineteen-year-old son, Frank Jr. (He was released unharmed two days later after a $240,000 ransom was paid; the kidnappers and virtually all of the money were picked up a couple of days later.) Toward the end of the decade, January 24, 1969, Frank lost his father Marty.

Frank would turn fifty-five in 1971. His time had come, so he thought, to retire.

F riendship, fraternity, bonhomie, esprit de corps, independence, lady-slaying, hell-raising, boozing, brawling, clowning—the Rat Pack had all this and more.

The term "Rat Pack" first cropped up in popular culture in the mid-fifties, when Lauren Bacall commented to her husband Humphrey Bogart, Frank, and friends that they looked "like a goddamn rat pack" after days of partying. Bogart seized the monicker and applied it enthusiastically to a group of friends who lived in the Holmby Hills area of Los Angeles and partied together: Judy Garland and her husband Sid Luft; agent Irving "Swifty" Lazar; writer Nathaniel Benchley; actor David Niven and his wife Hjordis; restaurateur Mike Romanoff and his wife Gloria; and songwriter Jimmy Van Heusen. (Unofficial part-timers included Dean Martin and his wife Jeanne; Spencer Tracy; Sammy Davis Jr.; Tony Curtis and his wife Janet Leigh; Clifton Webb; and Noel Coward.) Because of his rogue behavior, his nighttime stamina, his outrageous practical jokes, and his hipster lingo adapted by the others, Frank became "Pack Master" or "King Rat." Other monikers for him were the "Pope" and the "General." Bogart, always good for a lively quote, gleefully claimed that the Pack existed solely "for the relief of boredom and the perpetuation of independence. We admire ourselves and don't care for anyone else." It was all in fun, though there were some in Hollywood who criticized them for their licentious image and liberal politics. But when Bogart died of cancer in January 1957, the original Rat Pack died with him.

The new Rat Pack flourished as a group in the early sixties. The core of the Pack was Frank, Dean Martin, Sammy Davis Jr., Peter Lawford, and Joey Bishop. Others, such as Tony Curtis and Janet Leigh, Kirk Douglas, Steve Lawrence, Don Rickles, Robert Wagner, and Jimmy Van Heusen, were considered honorary members. Shirley MacLaine and Angie Dickinson—each considered "one of the guys"—were part of the scene, more official "mascots" than members. Hangers-on would also come and go throughout the years, empowered by association with Frank and company. But there was one important difference in the new Rat Pack: where the original was a group of equals, this one had only one leader—Sinatra.

140

Winners

The Rat Pack

"Here's to the winners, lift up the glasses . . ."

While filming *Ocean's Eleven* in January 1960, the core group appeared two nights a week at the Sands in Las Vegas, singing and joking together in a raucous, no-holds-barred, unrehearsed act that was more inpromptu onstage party (complete with rolling bar cart) than scripted show. Guest stars such as Shirley MacLaine, Bob Hope, and Milton Berle often made unannounced appearances, happy to be part of the buzz. The crowds were standing room only at this, the Pack's coming-out party. The Rat Packers acted together in other movies, becoming more and more associated together in the public's mind. All five also appeared in *Sergeants 3* in 1962. Frank and Dean again acted together in *4 for Texas* in 1963; Frank, Dean, and Sammy appeared together in *Robin and the Seven Hoods* in 1964.

For a time, the press referred to the group as the "Clan," but that word had overtones of the Ku Klux Klan; the Rat Packers themselves preferred the "Summit." But there was no shaking the name Bacall had come up—the Rat Pack—and that was what they were known as by the press. Meanwhile, the term "Ring-a-ding-ding," expressing a devil-may-care attitude with a touch of arrogance, became a catch phrase for the Rat Pack. Frank used it as the name of his first Reprise album in 1961, further codifying the Rat Pack philosophy.

Dean Martin, born Dino Paul Crocetti in Ohio, was sometimes (though not often) considered the co-leader of the Rat Pack. He and Frank had much in common: Italian-American ancestry, a career in both music and film (Martin co-starred in sixteen movies with Jerry Lewis in the 1940s and 1950s), and a devil-may-care approach to life. Dean (or "Dag" as Frank called him, short for "Dago") was considerably less mercurial than Frank and a good balance for his volatile nature. Frank first saw Dean perform with Jerry Lewis at the Copa in 1948. Frank and Martin performed together onstage in the fifties, but they didn't work together in movies until *Some Came Running* in 1958, released the same year as Martin's first dramatic role in his comeback picture, *The Young Lions*. Martin became Frank's most frequent co-star, appearing in the Rat Pack movies as well as *Come Blow Your Horn* (1963) and *Marriage on the Rocks* (1965). They both made a cameo appearance in *Pepe* (1960) and *Cannonball Run II* (1983).

Previous page: Peter Lawford and Sinatra, late forties.
The two starred together in *It Happened in Brooklyn* (1947).

Above: The Pack—Lawford, Dean Martin, Sammy Davis Jr., Sinatra.

"Frank and I are brothers, right? We cut the top of our thumbs and became blood brothers.

He wanted to cut the wrist. I said, 'What are you crazy?' No, here's good enough."

—Dean Martin

146

Sammy Davis Jr., singer, dancer, and powerhouse performer, added some electricity to the laid-back screen demeanor of Frank and Dean. In May 1947, Frank recommended a dance act of Will Mastin, his brother Sammy Davis Sr., and nephew Sammy Davis Jr.—who had been performing since age two—to open for him at the Capitol Theater in New York City; the salary of $1,250 a week was more than the dance trio had ever received. That was the start of a lifetime friendship between Sinatra and Davis, the versatile entertainer who Frank called Smokey because he smoked so much. Frank helped Davis land jobs in establishments that refused to hire or underpaid black performers. He also helped Davis through the trauma of losing an eye in a car accident in November 1954 with encouragement and humor. Frank was the best man at the wedding of Davis and actress Mai Britt on November 13, 1960. Davis acted in three of the four major Rat Pack movies and made cameo appearances with Frank in *Pepe* (1960) and *Cannonball Run II* (1960).

British-born Peter Lawford was the tamest of the Rat Pack. He had to be, since he had married into the Kennedy clan. Perhaps entertainers could carouse openly, but politicians and their families had to be discreet. Frank met Peter Lawford in April 1944, when both were working for MGM. Ten years later, on April 24, 1954, Lawford married Patricia Kennedy, a younger sister to John F. Kennedy. Frank and Lawford campaigned together on behalf of JFK in his 1960 run for the presidency and partied together with the President. It often was left to Lawford to clean up Rat Pack messes. Lawford worked on a number of film projects with Frank in addition to the Rat Pack movies *Ocean's Eleven* and *Sergeants 3*, including *It Happened in Brooklyn* (1947), *Never So Few* (1959), *Pepe* (1960), *The Oscar* (1966), and *That's Entertainment* (1974).

Comedian Joey Bishop (Joseph Abraham Gottlieb) was born in the Bronx and grew up in South Philadelphia. After catching his act at the Latin Quarter in Manhattan, Frank asked him to open up for him at the Riviera in Englewood, New Jersey, in September 1953. Bishop's deadpan delivery complemented the stage antics of Frank, Dean, and Sammy. He wrote many of the others' stage "ad-libs." Bishop appeared in *Ocean's Eleven*, *Sergeants 3*, and *Pepe* with the other Rat Packers.

Left: Sinatra, Martin, Davis, Lawford, and Joey Bishop in a publicity pose for *Ocean's Eleven* (1960).

Next page: The original Holmby Hills Rat Pack at Hollywood's Copa Room, 1956: (clockwise from bottom left) Humphrey Bogart, producer Sid Luft, Lauren Bacall, Judy Garland, model Ellie Graham, agent Jack Entratter, restaurateur Mike Romanoff, Sinatra, Mrs. Romanoff, David Niven, and Mrs. Niven.

Above: Dean Martin and Golden Nugget chairman Steve Wynn in
Atlantic City in the early eighties.

Overleaf: Davis, Sinatra, Shirley MacLaine, and Martin at
an early-eighties Friars Roast.

The Rat Pack and their hedonistic, party-till-you-drop way, their inside lingo, and their timeless sense of sartorial style, still capture the public's imagination. The term crops up all over popular culture; the nineties' retro celebration of cocktail culture once again put the Pack at the center of popular style. Yes, part of the ongoing fascination is nostalgia, and the classic yearning for a more innocent time full of fun and devoid of consequences. But equally important is the longing for self-expression, vigor, and bravado in the face of an uncertain future that the Rat Pack championed. Frank and Company operated in a less politically correct time when men were men and acted like it with little regard for the feelings of others. Selfish, to be sure, but ever so attractive.

Left: Martin and Sinatra performing at the Westchester Playhouse in the New York suburbs, early eighties.

Above: Visiting backstage with Davis during Sammy's early-sixties run in *Golden Boy* on Broadway.

High Hopes

Politics

"He's got high apple-pie-in-the-sky hopes . . ."

F rank Sinatra changed forever the way entertainers and politicians related to each other. Before him, the two rarely mixed. Stars avoided partisanship, and politicians thought show people beneath them. Sinatra was the first to connect the two worlds significantly—and oh so publicly.

Frank had been a public supporter of the Democratic party—or at least their presidential candidates—for many years. He enjoyed the limelight. He also was empowered by helping shape the nation's leadership. But part of him appreciated the simple fact of being an engaged citizen. He took advantage of his high-profile career in music and movies to make a contribution in the political arena. He could glad-hand with the best of them and would have made a dazzling candidate. But he chose to work on behalf of others, and to a certain extent he had an impact on the course of American history.

Frank grew up around politics. He accompanied his mother, a Democratic ward leader, to political events as a boy, and he sang at party meetings as a young man. As his career took off, he sought ways to channel a streak of political activism. In May 1942, while he was enjoying success as part of the Tommy Dorsey band, Frank ordered that a hundred medallions with a St. Christopher medal on one side and a Star of David on the other be made up as a personal response to stories of Nazi atrocities, and he gave them to friends. His actions and words had great influence, he came to realize, especially after he had become a solo phenomenon. Social activism also led to his participation in the movie short *The House I Live In* (1945), in which he encouraged America's youth to show racial and religious tolerance.

Frank named his son after President Franklin Delano Roosevelt (not Francis after himself, so the Frank Jr. is not entirely accurate). After Frank visited the White House and chatted with FDR over tea in September 1944, he decided to play a role in presidential politics. He publicly announced his support for Roosevelt's re-election. Some of Frank's fans began wearing buttons that said "Frankie's for FDR and so are we" (although many of his fans in the early days were too young to vote). Years later, in February 1960, Frank invited First Lady Eleanor Roosevelt on a television special and sat with her to talk about "hope" for the future.

Previous page and left: Sinatra with President and Nancy Reagan at the 1980 inauguration.

Overleaf: Lillian Carter, President Jimmy Carter's mother, with Frank at his seventy-fifth birthday celebration in Las Vegas.

Frank kept his hand in politics throughout the years, voting as a liberal Democrat and making sizable campaign contributions. He publicly supported Harry Truman over Thomas Dewey in 1948, and he was "Madly for Adlai" in Adlai Stevenson's unsuccessful bids to defeat Dwight D. Eisenhower in 1952 and 1956. In August 1956, Frank sang the National Anthem at the Democratic Convention.

On September 19, 1959, Sinatra hosted a luncheon of 400 Hollywood personalities in honor of Soviet premier Nikita Krushchev. In one of his shining hours, a charming Frank spread a message of goodwill and encouraged disarmament and rapprochement with Soviet Russia.

Sinatra played his most active political role on behalf of John F. Kennedy ("Chicky-Baby," Frank called him). In February 1960, when JFK was seeking the Democratic nomination in his bid for the presidency, his father Joseph Kennedy met with Frank and Peter Lawford about helping raise support among Catholic voters, asking Frank to enlist Chicago capo Sam Giancana's help. At Frank's request, Giancana dispatched his people to organize the coal miners' union in West Virginia, thus delivering crucial votes. Frank also used his mother's former political connections and his own influence to sway the New Jersey party apparatus in favor of JFK's candidacy.

During the campaign, Frank backed down on a personal issue on JFK's behalf. He had hired Albert Maltz, the writer of *The House I Live In*, to write a screenplay based on the book *The Execution of Private Slovik* (an account of the only American soldier executed for desertion since the Civil War). But Maltz had been one of Hollywood's blacklisted writers during Senator Joseph McCarthy's era and had been jailed for refusing to cooperate with the House Un-American Activities Committee. Frank's screenwriting offer was Maltz' first since 1948. Yet the press—in particular Hearst columnists—accused Frank once again of being soft on Communism. But Sinatra wanted to break the blacklist, and he stood firm under a massive outpouring of "Red or dead" vitriol from Hollywood stars such as John Wayne and William Holden, the Catholic Church, veterans' groups, family, friends, politicians, and even corporate sponsors of his TV show.

Above: Sinatra with New York Mayor Edward Koch
and violinist Isaac Stern.

Overleaf: The 1980 presidential inauguration.

It was only when Joseph Kennedy, worried how this might impact voters, telephoned Frank and told him the Kennedys wouldn't want his support if he hired Maltz that he bowed to overwhelming pressure. Frank gave Maltz the full amount he had promised him, $75,000— now not to write the screenplay—and abandoned the project entirely.

Once JFK won the nomination, Frank, along with Dean Martin and Sammy Davis Jr., performed fund-raising concerts. (Frank called the Rat Pack the "Jack Pack" for a time.) Frank even re-recorded the song "High Hopes" with pro-Kennedy lyrics by Sammy Cahn. He helped mobilize support in Chicago, again through Giancana; JFK carried the state by only 8,858 votes.

Frank, along with Lawford, was hired to produce JFK's inaugural ball in January 1961. Among the performers were Harry Belafonte, Milton Berle, Leonard Bernstein, Joey Bishop, Nat King Cole, Jimmy Durante, Ella Fitzgerald, Mahalia Jackson, Gene Kelly, Ethel Merman, Laurence Olivier, Sidney Poitier, and Anthony Quinn. (But not Sammy Davis Jr., much to Frank's dismay, because there were those who were worried that the participation of a black man who was married to a white woman would alienate the public.) Frank escorted Jacqueline Kennedy to the inaugural gala and sang himself.

These were heady times for Frank. Yet Frank's reputation as a friend to Giancana and other mobsters concerned JFK's advisors—especially his brother Robert F. Kennedy, the Attorney General. The fact that JFK and Frank had shared women—notably Marilyn Monroe and Judith Exner Campbell (who also had been intimate with Giancana)—also was a cause for concern. They advised the President to distance himself from Frank. In February 1962, on a visit to Palm Springs, JFK canceled his plans to stay at Frank's home and stayed with Bing Crosby instead, a diehard Republican. The official story was that the Secret Service considered Crosby's home more secure because, unlike Frank's, it stood up against a mountain. Yet Frank considered the change of plans a personal snub and blamed Bobby.

Left: Sinatra accepts a plaque from Jerusalem Mayor Teddy Kollek.

Above: In Egypt at a children's benefit concert with Anwar Sadat, president of Egypt.

Frank supported Lyndon Johnson over the Republican candidate Barry Goldwater in 1964, but with nothing like the commitment he had given to the Kennedy cause. In 1968, he chose Vice President Hubert Humphrey as his candidate over now-senator Robert Kennedy, breaking with some of his liberal friends, such as Sammy Davis Jr. and Shirley MacLaine, who opposed the war in Vietnam. Frank genuinely liked Humphrey, but his support of his candidacy may have been affected by his mixed feelings for Bobby (although Frank's view had softened somewhat when Bobby personally offered the FBI's help during Frank Jr.'s kidnapping soon after JFK's assassination). In any case, some of Humphrey's advisors had reservations about Frank's involvement, again due to Frank's reputed associates, and Frank ended up keeping a low profile in Humphrey's unsuccessful run for the White House.

In July 1970, Frank switched parties, announcing his support for Ronald Reagan in his run for the governorship of California. In July 1972, Frank announced his support for the re-election of President Richard Nixon over Senator George McGovern, even though his daughter Tina was a campaign worker for McGovern. The following August, Frank attended the Republican National Convention and, after Nixon's election victory, performed at the White House in April 1973. Nixon's vice president, Spiro Agnew, was a frequent guest at Frank's home in Palm Springs.

In 1976, Frank announced his support for Gerald Ford over Jimmy Carter. In 1980, Frank and Dean Martin performed on behalf of Ronald Reagan's presidential campaign against President Jimmy Carter, raising about half a million. After the election he produced and sang at Reagan's inaugural gala, just as he had for JFK.

Frank's political philosophy, he explained, had evolved from support of defending the rights of the "little guy"— a Democratic Party tenet—to populism against big government's oppression of the "little guy," a Republican Party doctrine. Regardless of his affiliation, though, Sinatra was somewhat of a kingmaker for almost half a century. The relationship between Hollywood and Washington would never be the same.

Left: The 1980 presidential inauguration.

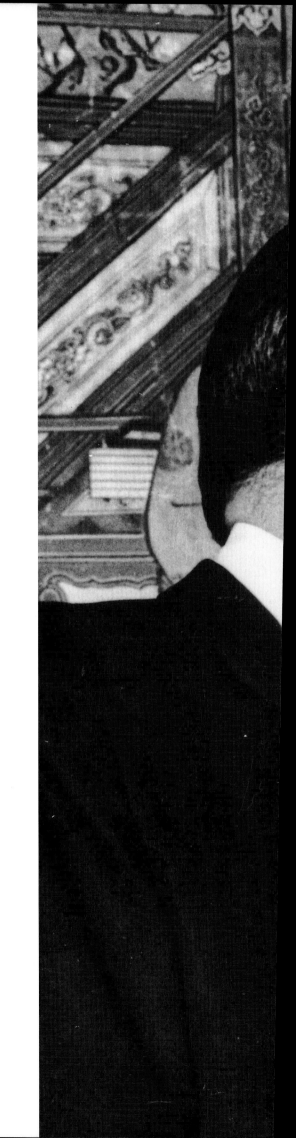

rank met Mia Farrow (Maria de Lourdes Villiers Farrow) in October 1964 on the 20th Century-Fox lot, after he had returned from Europe to film interiors for *Von Ryan's Express*. She was taping the television show *Peyton Place* at a neighboring sound stage. One day as Sinatra and company left his stage after a day's work, he noticed a slender vision of a girl at the door. She wore a gauzy, ankle-length nightgown that the sun streamed through, and her long blonde hair shimmered. She smiled at him.

That went on for a week. At the end of every day she would appear at his sound-stage door, in the nightgown she had borrowed from wardrobe. At the end of the week, he asked her if she'd like to fly to Palm Springs with him for the weekend. So began an affair that would lead to marriage, her first of course, his third.

Frank was pushing fifty. She was nineteen, five years younger than his daughter Nancy. Yet she'd had a life chock-full of experience. The daughter of director John Farrow and actress Maureen O'Sullivan (Jane to Johnny Weissmuller's Tarzan), she had battled polio at age nine, been kicked out of two convent schools for independent thinking by age ten, and acted on stage and in film at fourteen. After landing a role in an off-Broadway revival of *The Importance of Being Earnest*, she was picked to play the female lead in *Peyton Place*, the TV series based on the huge bestseller by Grace Metalious. The show was an instant hit, and Mia was a television star at the tender age of nineteen.

Their next date was a screening of the film *None But the Brave*, which Frank had directed. They soon began spending more weekends together at Frank's Palm Springs home; then it was holidays together. In August 1965, Frank took Mia on a cruise on a chartered yacht along the East Coast, stopping to visit the Kennedys at Hyannisport. The tabloids tracked their every move.

You Make Me Feel So Young

Mia

"You make me feel there are songs to be sung . . ."

Their temperaments were different. He came off as self-assured, all-powerful, and volatile; she acted insecure, vulnerable, and even-tempered. Their lifestyles were different too. He was a heavy drinker, always on the move; she was a smoker of marijuana and meditative. Her taste in music favored the Beatles more than Frank's work. A sixties spirit, she opposed the Vietnam War and dressed down; he was a member of an older, pressed-trousers-and-cardigan generation and had never owned a pair of jeans in his life. But each had something the other thought they wanted. He was attempting to control his rages, which kept getting him into trouble. She sought greater confidence in life. He wanted to be more introspective; she wanted to become more outgoing. In any case, their time together was intense and passionate.

The highly charged relationship at times turned stormy over the next months. One fight was over Frank not wanting to embarrass his mother by bringing Mia to his fiftieth birthday party. (She didn't attend.) Then, on July 4, 1966, Frank presented Mia with a nine-carat engagement ring worth $85,000. The next day, he left for London to begin filming *The Naked Runner*. A few days later, Frank decided he couldn't wait. He called a friend at the Sands in Las Vegas and told him to take care of the details: the marriage certificate, a judge, the cake, and champagne. He called Mia, jumped on his private plane, and flew to New York and then Las Vegas. There, in a private ceremony on July 19, 1966, a nervous Frank slipped a gold band on Mia's finger and kissed her three times. The judge pronounced them man and wife. The newlyweds flew to New York and then London so Frank could finish the movie shoot.

That August, they bought a house together in Bel Air and began renovations to the Palm Springs home, adding a tennis court, bungalow, and guesthouse. They were the picture of true love.

"He was just so . . . so . . . cool."

—Mia Farrow

Previous page: Sinatra and Mia Farrow on the luxury yacht *Southern Breeze* in the harbor at Edgartown, Massachusetts, August 5, 1965.

Right and chapter title page: The wedding, July 19, 1966.

Above: With Mia Farrow in Miami, January 1967.

But it wasn't long before cracks began to appear. Their efforts to build a life together kept getting sidetracked by their differences—some of which only grew more pronounced: their disparate views on Vietnam; Frank's destructive behavior when partying with his buddies; Mia's insensitivity to him in letting herself be photographed with other men (dancing with Bobby Kennedy at a Los Angeles nightclub, for instance). What finally caused a separation sixteen months later, in November 1967, was the question of who was master of her career. Frank would have preferred she didn't work at all—he didn't want a repeat of his experience with Ava, when they found themselves on different continents during film projects. He had reached a compromise with Mia that she make only one film a year. But when she refused to walk off the set of the behind-schedule *Rosemary's Baby* (a practice he was famous for), to star with him in *The Detective*, it was the final straw. He decided he had to end his relationship with her and had her served with divorce papers during her shoot.

Mia didn't want to give up on the relationship and begged Frank to take her back. They spent that Christmas together in one last attempt at a reconciliation, but it was too little too late. Their differences were too painfully obvious. After the holiday Mia flew to the Himalayas to meditate with her guru.

The early part of 1968 was hard on both of them. The pain of the divorce hit Frank harder than he or his friends had expected; he pined for her over several months, but he'd given up in his heart trying to make it work. The divorce was finalized in August 1968. Mia refused the offer of a generous alimony; all she wanted, she said, was his friendship. She kept the jewelry and silverware he'd given her and moved out of their Bel-Air home.

Frank had a lot of living to do—and a lot of loving as well. And as for marriage, well, for Frank the fourth time would be the charm.

The Last Dance

The First Retirement

"It's the last song . . ."

Frank Sinatra turned fifty-five on December 15, 1970. He had climbed the mountain to the top of the entertainment world, fallen off, then climbed an even higher peak. He was the most acclaimed singer of his time. With his selection and interpretation of songs, he had made an incomparable contribution to the history of American music. Moreover, he'd forged a successful film and television career and had even won the most prestigious award in film acting, an Oscar.

Sinatra's personal life had been as full as his professional career. He had been married three times. From his first marriage, he had three children with whom he had strong relationships. He'd had many intense romances. He had many close friends with whom he had partied into the night time and again. He had traveled all over the world. He had met and influenced world leaders. And he had more money that he'd ever be able to spend. In the song that the public came to regard as his personal anthem, "My Way," recorded on December 30, 1968, he sang, "And so I face the final curtain."

The death of seventy-four-year-old Marty Sinatra from heart complications on January 24, 1969, had an enormous impact on Frank. Though it was expected— he'd been ill for several years—the devoted son was shaken to the core, and became acutely aware of his own mortality. He had come to rely on his father's quiet strength and wisdom for solace in the whirlwind that was his life. And he realized how important it was that he be accessible to his own children.

Frank also was exhausted—too many hours on the road, too many late nights, too many movies. He wanted to slow down, reflect and read and write and even paint. Sales of his albums had slowed down in competition with rock music. His latest movie, *Dirty Dingus Magee*, a western comedy released in 1970, had been received poorly. His last few albums had sold miserably. Was it time to get out of the game?

Left: Sinatra and Harry James in June 1979 performing "All or Nothing at All," forty years after their original recording.

"People like my father are always looking for ways to express their creative force. They find windows through their own souls through which they can shed their light. That force has to come out, and painting is one outlet."

—Tina Sinatra

Previous page: The Painter: Sinatra and self-portrait.

Left: The Photographer: A candid mid-seventies shot.

On March 23, 1971, Frank released a statement to the press in which he announced his retirement. He stated that he needed "a long pause in which to seek a better understanding of changes occurring in the world."

On April 15, 1971, Frank won the Jean Hersholt Humanitarian Award at the Oscars. This award, honoring the philanthropic work Frank had done as a public figure and private citizen, seemed a fitting conclusion to his long and storied career. Then on June 14, Frank gave what was to be his final performance—a benefit for the Motion Picture and Television Relief Fund at the Los Angeles Music Center. It was an evening to remember. His entire family, and many show-business friends were present, such as Jack Benny, Cary Grant, Don Rickles, and Rosalind Russell, as well as political friends, the governor of California, Ronald Reagan, and his wife Nancy, Vice President Spiro Agnew and his wife, and President Nixon's advisor Henry Kissinger.

Frank sang some of his most famous songs: "All or Nothing at All," "I've Got You Under My Skin," "I'll Never Smile Again," "Nancy," "Fly Me to the Moon," "The Lady Is a Tramp," "Ol' Man River," "My Way," and "That's Life." He sang about the old days and told stories about them. There were frequent standing ovations. Then is was time for his final encore. "I've built my career on saloon songs," he said, then slid into the melancholy "Angel Eyes." A pin spotlight illuminated his face. Halfway into the song he lit a cigarette, smoke rising around him. He sang the song's last line: " 'Scuse me while I disappear." The lights went down. When they came back up, he was gone.

In *Life* magazine's June 25 cover story about Frank's retirement, "Sinatra Says Good-Bye and Amen: A farewell to 30 very good years," Tommy Thompson wrote: "It was the single most stunning moment I have ever witnessed on stage."

How Do You Keep the Music Playing?

Ol' Blue Eyes Is Back

"The music never ends . . ."

S inatra's retirement was an active one. He spent time with his children. He painted with oils in his Palm Springs studio. He studied current events. He performed charity work. He campaigned for his chosen presidential candidate, supporting the re-election of President Richard Nixon over Senator George McGovern in 1972. He played golf.

But Frank missed the music—and the applause. And his fans, through thousands of letters, reminded him how much they too missed his music. On May 26, 1973, the Songwriters of America selected Sinatra as the "Entertainer of the Century." But was that it? Would Frank spend the rest of the century looking back on his artistic contributions, his voice silent?

Not for long.

Sinatra returned to the studio in June 1973 to record the album *Ol' Blue Eyes Is Back*. That September, he taped a television special of the same name—a "retirement from retirement." Filmed in front of a black-tie on-camera audience, and featuring the arrangements of conductors Gordon Jenkins (for the ballads) and Don Costa (for the swing tunes), the one-hour show aired on NBC on Sunday, November 18, 1973. Frank's features had filled out; his voice was grainier; and with shorter wind, he depended more and more on syncopation—and twenty extra violins in the orchestra—to handle a song. But as always, his phrasing was impeccable and the emotional content authentic. The show itself scored disappointing ratings, but rhapsodic reviews from the press made it clear that the Chairman was back on board.

Frank committed himself to this second "comeback" with numerous concert appearances. He returned to Las Vegas to play Caesars Palace before a crowd packed with celebrities. His Main Event tour, presented with the boxing theme of the "world champion" in the ring, drew crowds of up to 40,000 and climaxed in a televised concert at New York City's Madison Square Garden on October 13, 1974. The legend was back and going strong.

Above: With Bob Hope at a rehearsal at the 1980 presidential inauguration.

Left: Ol' Blue Eyes, mid-eighties.

Frank returned to the movies as well. He co-hosted *That's Entertainment* (1974) and *That's Entertainment Part II* (1976), sterling documentaries about MGM musicals. On November 19, 1977, Frank appeared on NBC in the made-for-television movie *Contract on Cherry Street* as a New York City police officer.

During the 1970s, Frank experienced the joy of becoming a grandparent. On May 22, 1974, his daughter Nancy gave birth to Angela Jennifer Lambert. A second granddaughter, Amanda Katherine Lambert, was born on March 17, 1976. He also married for the fourth time on July 11, 1976, to Barbara Marx, the ex-wife of Zeppo Marx (of the Marx Brothers), a Palm Springs neighbor. But Frank also suffered the loss of his mother Dolly, who was killed in a plane crash on January 6, 1977, on a flight from Palm Springs to attend opening night of one of Frank's Las Vegas shows. In the middle of a blinding low-altitude snowstorm, the chartered Learjet carrying Dolly and a female friend crashed into the side of the highest mountain in California, an 11,502-foot peak in the San Gorgonio range.

His mother's death devastated Sinatra, and he was inconsolable for quite some time. Yet he forced himself to keep working.

A rite of passage occurred March 14, 1977, when Frank participated in his final session with Nelson Riddle, recording the songs "Linda," "Sweet Lorraine," and a vocal overdub of "Barbara." On January 26, 1980, Frank appeared in Rio de Janeiro before the largest paying audience—some 175,000 people—ever to attend a concert by a solo performer to that time. The following March, he released the ambitious three-disc album *Trilogy*. It went to the top of the charts and received six Grammy nominations. He also received good notices for his role as a detective in the feature film *The First Deadly Sin*, released that October.

While keeping up a busy concert schedule and appearing sporadically on television and in cameo performances on film in the 1980s, Frank continued charity and political work. In December 1983, he received the Lifetime Achievement Award from the Kennedy Center.

Above: Sinatra and Paul Anka after a benefit show
for the Memorial Sloan-Kettering Cancer Center in the late seventies.

Above: Backstage with Luciano Pavarotti at the Uris Theater
in New York City in the late seventies.

Above: Donald and Ivana Trump, Barbara and Frank Sinatra, and Kitty Carlisle.

Left: With Harry James in Las Vegas in the late seventies.

Above: With Dionne Warwick at a Friars Roast in the early eighties.

Overleaf: Rich Little, Bob Hope, Johnny Carson, Sinatra, and Ben Vereen at a rehearsal for the 1980 presidental inauguration.

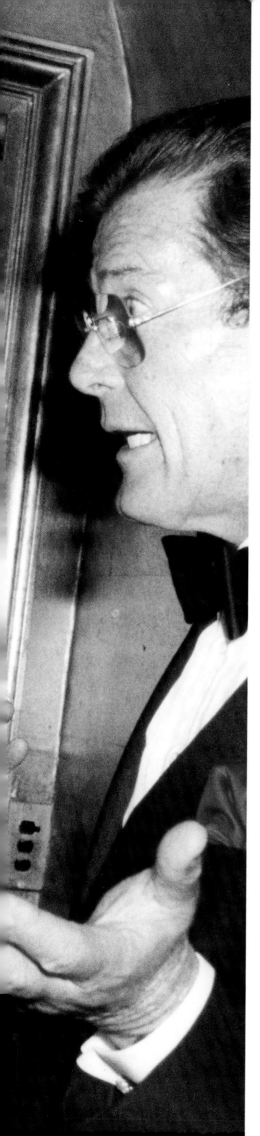

The *Sinatra Suite*, a dance choreographed by Twyla Tharp to "All the Way," "That's Life," "My Way," and "One for My Baby," was performed in his honor by Mikhail Baryshnikov and Elaine Kudo. In January 1985, Frank produced President Ronald Reagan's inaugural ball. In May 1985, he was presented the Medal of Freedom by President Reagan. That same month, he received an honorary degree from Stevens Institute of Technology, an engineering school in his hometown of Hoboken (which his parents had once hoped he would attend).

In March 1988, Frank, Dean Martin, and Sammy Davis Jr. began a reunion tour. Dean had recently lost his son Dino in a plane crash, and Frank conceived of the tour primarily as a way to get Martin over his grief. But Dean left the tour before it ended—he just couldn't conquer the depression. In 1989, Frank toured with Sammy and Liza Minnelli, as well as on his own. Most concerts sold out.

Frank, in his seventies, was going strong.

Frank Sinatra

Duets-II

Left: Sammy Davis Jr., Sinatra, and Roger Moore.

It All Depends on You

Barbara Marx

"Isn't it sweet to know, dear,
you can help me on? ..."

Barbara Jane Blakeley was born in Glendale, California, in 1930, moving to Wichita, Kansas, with her family for a time, then to Long Beach, California. Tall, slender, and blond, she won several beauty pageants and, at age twenty-one, she founded the Barbara Blakeley School of Modeling and Charm. She married Robert Harrison Oliver, who worked for the Miss Universe Beauty Pageant, and had a son Bobby by him. After divorcing Oliver, she began a new career as a Las Vegas showgirl, during which time she met Zeppo Marx of the Marx Brothers. They married in 1959 and lived in Palm Springs, neighbors of Sinatra. By 1972, her marriage was in trouble. Frank and Barbara started dating that year. She filed for a divorce from Zeppo in December. The following January, she accompanied Frank to Richard Nixon's inauguration.

During the three-and-a-half years that Frank dated Barbara, he had other flings, notably with actress Carol Lynley. Also, at the time of an engagement at the Uris Theater in September 1975 with Count Basie and Ella Fitzgerald, he had a rendezvous with Jacqueline Kennedy Onassis. (Jackie had lost her second husband, Aristotle Onassis, a year and a half earlier.) Following his performance, Frank and Jackie went to the 21 Club and then to his suite at the Waldorf Towers. After this date, Jackie refused all contact with Frank despite his repeated efforts. It has been reported that Ethel Kennedy, widow of Bobby, informed her that Frank had introduced President Kennedy to Judith Exner Campbell and other women with whom her first husband had had affairs, and that a relationship with Frank Sinatra would upset the family.

In May 1976, Frank proposed to Barbara Marx. She was everything he needed at this time of his life— devoted, organized, a homemaker, someone to look after him. Frank's decision to remarry for the fourth time was difficult on his children, who had become closer to their father with his advancing years. But they adjusted to his new relationship. Dolly Sinatra, always outspoken, also resisted the union, but eventually agreed to attend the ceremony.

Above: Barbara and Frank Sinatra and Time Warner chairman Steve Ross and wife
at an early eighties Police Athletic League dinner honoring Ross.

Left: Frank and a playful Barbara enjoy a dinner party at the Waldorf Astoria in April, 1977
after a Sinatra-Robert Merrill benefit concert at Carnegie Hall.

"He turns every day into Christmas.
It knocks me out. Maybe I appreciate it more
because I didn't always have it."

–Barbara Marx Sinatra

Above: Steve Wynn, Frank, and Barbara celebrate Sinatra's seventy-fifth birthday
at the Golden Nugget in Atlantic City.

Above: Agent Irving "Swifty" Lazar, author Judy Green, Frank, and Barbara.

Right: Frank and Barbara in their Palm Springs home, 1977.

"I really have found some kind of wonderful tranquility. What the hell, it's about time. I'm at a very happy part in life. Barbara is a marvelous woman, a great gal."

—Frank Sinatra

Above: At the third game of the 1977 World Series in Los Angeles.

Frank and Barbara were married on July 11, 1976, in Rancho Mirage, California, at Sunnylands, the estate of Walter Annenberg, publisher of *TV Guide*. The affair was a top-secret one; the 120 invited guests weren't even sure it was to be a wedding, since the invitations had mentioned an "engagement party," and Frank had announced that they would be married the following October at the home of Kirk Douglas. The sixty-year-old bridegroom and the forty-six-year-old bride were married a little after 3:00 p.m.

Frank later decided to have a second Catholic ceremony. In order to do so, he had to have his marriage to Nancy Barbato Sinatra annulled by the Catholic Church. The death of his mother in an airplane crash on January 6, 1977, had made Frank more religious and he supported the idea despite the protestations of his children who thought such an action was a slight to their mother.

Frank had found a loyal wife for his sunset years, someone to watch over him. His marriage to Barbara would last longer than all the others combined.

Too Marvelous for Words

Fatherhood

"You're much too much,
and just too very very . . ."

Frank Sinatra experienced the joys of parenting in his first marriage. By Nancy Barbato Sinatra, he had three beautiful children: Nancy Sandra, born on June 8, 1940; Franklin Wayne Emmanuel (Frank Jr. or Frankie), born on January 10, 1944; and Christina (Tina), born on June 20, 1948.

His children provided Sinatra with an anchor during his stormy times. Their devotion to him as well as his concerns for them gave him perspective on the rigors of his career. But fatherhood created new problems too. It made his breakup with their mother all the more heart-wrenching. It meant that there were three more people to whom he had to explain his life choices—such as remarrying three more times. And it meant that he had to worry about the safety and well-being of others. As it turned out, Frank would learn that even after they had made it through adolescence, they were still in harm's way as his children.

Frank missed much of his children's early years because of his career, his restlessness, and his divorce from their mother. When he did see them, he tried to make up for his time away from them with lavish gifts. Later in life, he and his children developed professional relationships beyond familial ties.

Nancy Sinatra grew up with dreams of singing, dancing, and acting. She attended the University of Southern California for one semester, then dropped out to pursue a career in entertainment. She made her television debut on her father's ABC television special *The Frank Sinatra-Timex Special: Welcome Home Elvis*, which aired on May 12, 1960. Her breakthrough was in rock'n'roll, with her first releases doing well in Europe and South Africa. In 1965, her song "These Boots Are Made for Walking" became a number-one hit in the United States. "Sugar Town" also went gold, as did the duet with her father, "Somethin' Stupid," in 1967. She also had several hits with songwriter-singer Lee Hazelwood.

Left: Frank with three-year-old Nancy, 1943.

"My kids are lucky...but it's more than that. Their mother, Nancy, has raised them beautifully. She's given them their character, their poise, their ability to adjust. She's been wonderful. Without the background she gave them, the good things might not have happened."

—Frank Sinatra

Nancy appeared in a number of movies, including *Marriage on the Rocks* with her father in 1965 and the Elvis Presley vehicle *Speedway* in 1968. She also wrote a book entitled *Frank Sinatra—My Father*, original published in 1985 (and then rewritten and republished as *Frank Sinatra—American Legend* in 1995). In 1995, Nancy made waves within the family by posing nude for *Playboy* magazine—though her father supported her, provided the money was right. For her it was a way to jumpstart her career and promote her new album *One More Time*.

Nancy married Tommy Sands—singer, television personality, and film actor—on September 11, 1960. They divorced five years later, a difficult time for her. She married producer Hugh Lambert on December 12, 1970, and bore him two daughters —Angela Jennifer (A.J.) Lambert on May 22, 1974, and Amanda Katherine Lambert on March 17, 1976. Hugh Lambert died of throat cancer in 1985 at the age of fifty-five.

Number-two child Frank Jr. demonstrated an aptitude for music when young. He mastered the piano as well as arranging. He attended the University of Southern California, but dropped out after a year to pursue his dream—music. For a time, he worked at Reprise Records. In September 1963, he launched his solo career at the Royal Box in the Americana Hotel in New York City. Later that year, he was hired to sing with the revamped Tommy Dorsey band. August 29, 1969 was a historic occasion for Frank's family—all three performing Sinatras were booked in Las Vegas: Frank at Caesars Palace, Nancy at the International Hilton, and Frank Jr. at the Frontier.

Frank Jr.'s performances improved steadily over the years, but his singing career never really got off the ground. In the late 1980s and early 1990s, he worked as Frank's musical director. Frank Jr. had a son, Michael Francis Sinatra, by Pat Fisher on March 1, 1987, making Frank a grandfather for the third time.

Left: Frank and family at a Los Angeles nightclub, 1943.

"Daddy is the most charismatic figure of the twentieth century."
–Nancy Sinatra

Above and left: Frank and Nancy.

Tina Sinatra was perhaps the most rebellious, especially politically. In 1972, when Frank supported the re-election of President Richard Nixon, she campaigned for George McGovern, even wearing a McGovern button into the Nixon White House on a visit there with her father. Tina edited and wrote the introduction for the book *A Man and His Art*, about Frank's paintings, published in 1991. She also wrote and produced the acclaimed five-hour CBS miniseries about her father's life through 1974, *Sinatra: The Music Was Just the Beginning*. The special aired in November 1992 and received excellent reviews, many of them surprised by how honest the film was.

For a time, at age twenty-three, Tina was engaged to the actor Robert Wagner, but they never married. She married record executive Wes Farrell on January 26, 1974, but the marriage lasted only eleven months. She married businessman Richard Cohen on January 30, 1981.

A parent's worst fears—in this case a celebrity parent's worst fears—came true for Frank in late 1963. Still reeling from the assassination of his friend President Kennedy sixteen days before, Frank learned on December 8, 1963, at about 9:30 p.m., that his only son had just been abducted.

Frank Jr. had just begun his musical career at age nineteen and had come to Lake Tahoe to perform at Harrah's Club with the Tommy Dorsey band. Twenty-three-year-old Barry Keenan had gone to both grade school and high school with Nancy and had visited the Sinatra household several times. A former stockbroker with a drug and drinking problem, he concocted a plan to kidnap the child of a celebrity to make a quick score of money, and he roped in his friends Joe Amsler and John Irwin to help him. At 9:30 in the evening, Keenan abducted Frank Jr. at gunpoint at Harrah's South Lodge, where the musicians were housed. He and Amsler tied up John Foss, a trumpet player, before taking Frank Jr. away. Foss soon freed himself, however, and before long Tino Barzie, Frank Jr.'s manager, had telephoned Nancy Barbato Sinatra at her home in Bel-Air, and she called Frank in Palm Springs.

Above and right: Frank and Frank Jr.

Overleaf: At a press conference following the 1963 kidnapping.

"*I love being a father and a grandfather. I love having the house full.*"

–*Frank Sinatra*

Above: Tina, Frank, and Nancy arrive at a Beverly Hills hotel
for his fiftieth birthday celebration in December 1965.

Thus began a two-and-a-half-day ordeal for the entire family. While waiting for contact, Frank received calls from FBI director J. Edgar Hoover and Attorney General Bobby Kennedy and even from Chicago mobster Sam Giancana, all offering help.

The first call from the kidnappers came at 4:45 p.m. the next day, December 9. Frank heard his son's voice, to his great relief. A series of other calls followed that day and the next. Frank eventually learned he was to have a courier drop off $240,000 in small bills at a gas station between two parked schoolbuses. The dropoff by FBI agent Jerome Crowe finally took place after 10:00 p.m. on December 10. Frank Jr. meanwhile was being held by John Irwin at a house in the San Fernando Valley. Arrangements broke down when the kidnappers became suspicious of one another. Irwin decided to let Frank Jr. go ahead of schedule and called the family four hours after the drop-off to say he had freed Frank Jr. on the San Diego Freeway at the Mulholland Drive exit. This was 2:00 a.m., the morning of December 11. By the time Frank and Crowe got there, however, Frank Jr. had fled. Frank, fearing the worst, was devastated. But Frank Jr. soon managed to stop a car of the Bel-Air Patrol, a private security company. To get Frank Jr. through the press surrounding the Sinatra home, the security man, George C. Jones, at Frank Jr.'s suggestion, drove him to his mother's home in his trunk. On opening the trunk, the family heard: "Hi, Mom. Hi, Dad."

The worst of the ordeal was over. The family still had to live through that suspenseful time until the kidnappers were captured. A tip from Amsler's brother as well as what Frank Jr. remembered of the kidnapping led to their arrest on December 14, and the recovery of the ransom money. At the trial the following February, the three defendants used a defense that further rocked the family–that Frank Jr. had staged the kidnapping for publicity purposes. (Keenan, now out of jail and a real estate developer, has publicly apologized for this legal tactic.) But the jury refused to believe the hoax claim and in short order found the three defendants guilty of kidnapping.

Frank lived through some bad times. But those several days during which time he didn't know whether his son would survive or not—when all that mattered was being a father and having a son—probably were the worst of all.

*I Thought
About You*

Humanitarian

"*That's what life's all about . . .*"

rank Sinatra's life was filled with many acts of generosity and kindness, large and small. He was a committed philanthropist as well as a dedicated friend.

During World War II, Sinatra helped the cause through non-profit events, such as a U.S. bond rally and a concert on behalf of Greek war relief. In January 1944, he performed a benefit for the Jewish Home for the Aged in Los Angeles. In May-June 1945, Frank traveled abroad to North Africa and Italy with comedian Phil Silvers to entertain U.S. troops.

Frank's social conscience further became evident to the public in September 1945 with the release of a movie short entitled *The House I Live In,* after a song of Frank's. All proceeds from the ten-minute movie, in which Frank speaks to a group of boys about racial and religious understanding, went to charity. The following November, as a follow-up to the movie, Frank toured schools and lectured on the subject of civil rights. *The House I Live In* earned Frank a special Oscar at the Academy Awards the following March.

Over the next several years, Frank performed at many charity events. In June 1958, for example, he performed in Monaco on behalf of the United Nations Fund for Refugee Children. He also appeared on behalf of smaller organizations, such as a sheriff's department or a hospital. In April-June 1962, Frank underwrote and participated in a World Tour for Children, with concerts in Hong Kong, Israel, Greece, Italy, England, France, and Monaco. He returned to Israel in July 1964 for the dedication of the Frank Sinatra International Youth Center for Arab and Jewish Children in Tel Aviv. That same month, he gave a benefit concert in San Francisco for the NAACP. In November 1966, he appeared in Las Vegas at a benefit for St. Jude's Children's Research Center, a charity supported by comedian Danny Thomas. The Frank Sinatra Child Care Unit was eventually established at St. Jude's in Memphis, Tennessee. Beginning in May 1967, Frank headed a national campaign for the America-Italian Anti-Defamation League. In June 1967, he performed at an all-star rally for the country of Israel at the Hollywood Bowl in Los Angeles.

Above: Sinatra accepts the Primum Vivere ("Life First") Award at the World Mercy Fund Ball, October 1979.

Right: Sinatra accepts a humanitarian award at New York City's Columbus Day Ball in 1979.

"If you say to Frank, 'I'm having a problem,'
it becomes his problem."

—Burt Lancaster

In August 1970, he again appeared at the Hollywood Bowl on behalf of Nos Ostros, a Hispanic-American charitable organization. Even Frank's "retirement" concert of June 14, 1971, was on behalf of the Motion Picture and Television Relief Fund.

During his retirement, Frank broadened the nature of his charitable work. In February-March 1972, for example, he co-sponsored a golf tournament with Arnold Palmer on behalf of the Tony Lema Scholarship Fund. And when he came out of retirement in late 1973, he again continued his frequent performances on behalf of charities. In April 1974, he toured for the Variety Clubs International, a children's charity. That September, he sang at a benefit concert to raise funds to build the Cedars-Sinai Medical Center. In August 1975, he made an appearance on Jerry Lewis's Telethon for Muscular Dystrophy. He again appeared on the Telethon a year later, in September 1976; this time, unknown to Jerry Lewis, he asked Dean Martin to accompany him. Martin and Lewis had not spoken for more than two decades, and Frank made it a personal cause to patch the broken friendship of these former partners. The result was a moving moment that only the magic of television can capture, as the two made up for lost time. In April 1977, Frank sang at a benefit in Palm Springs for the Friends of the Eisenhower Medical Center. He helped raise money for the University of Nevada in August. In April 1978, he again traveled to Israel for the dedication of the Frank Sinatra International Student Center at the Hebrew University.

Frank continued his good deeds for universities, hospitals, and charities into the 1980s. In January 1980, he began a three-year stint as campaign chairman for the National Multiple Sclerosis Society. A year later he performed the first of five concerts for The Memorial Sloan-Kettering Cancer Center, which raised nine million dollars for the Frank Sinatra Fund, for those unable to afford medical care. A wing was named after him.

"Frank was loyal above all else. With him, it was always loyalty first, thoughtfulness in a thousand ways."

–Gregory Peck

Right: The son of a fireman, Frank received several awards from firefighters for his charity work.

VARIETY CLUBS
INTERNATIONAL
Humanitarian Award
PRESENTED TO
FRANK SINATRA

1980

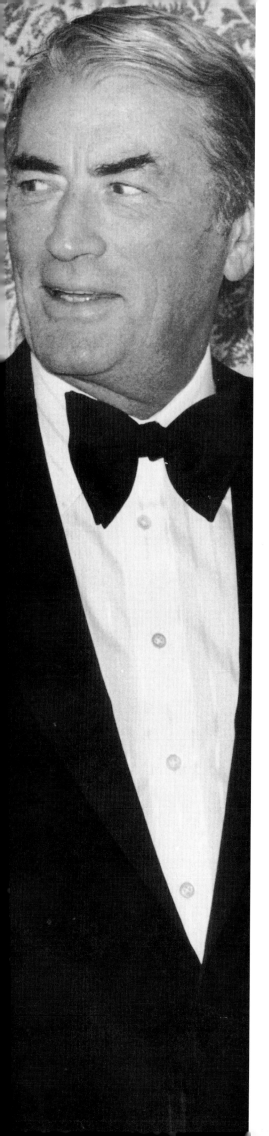

On November 20, 1983, at The Variety Club's All-Star Party, Frank was honored by other performers— among them Cary Grant, Carol Burnett, Milton Berle, Danny Thomas, Jimmy Stewart, and Richard Burton— for his fund-raising on behalf of the Seattle Children's Orthopedic Hospital. At that time, the Sinatra Family Children's Unit for the Chronically Ill was dedicated. In October 1984, Frank performed in Austria on behalf of that country's children charities. Two years later, in October 1986, the Barbara Sinatra Children's Center opened at the Eisenhower Medical Center in Rancho Mirage, California; Frank often acted as a fund-raiser for the center. One year later, in October 1987, he performed on behalf of the United Way. That November, he performed for the Juvenile Diabetes Foundation.

The list goes on and on. There are many organizations, large and small, not mentioned here that Frank supported through benefit performances. Especially in his later years he became the entertainer charities in need called first—his initial response was always "How much do you need?" or "When do you want me to appear?", and he always paid his own travel expenses on any charity trip. In addition, he made sizable donations, often anonymously, to countless charities. It has been estimated that Frank was responsible for raising and donating more than one billion dollars to charities.

But philanthropic or humanitarian work cannot be measured in dollars alone. An outspoken advocate of civil rights since the forties, Frank paid tribute to the Reverend Martin Luther King Jr. in 1961 by performing at a Carnegie Hall benefit for the Southern Christian Leadership Conference. And Frank took it upon himself to see that clubs treated Sammy Davis Jr. and other black performers with the same respect given to whites, insisting on bookings they'd never had at wages equal to those of white performers. It's no exaggeration to say that he helped change the nature of the entertainment business.

Left: Sinatra receives the 1980 Variety Clubs International Humanitarian Award from Princess Grace of Monaco and Gregory Peck.

Above: Frank receives an honorary Doctorate of Engineering
from Stevens Institute in Hoboken, New Jersey in 1985.

Sinatra also offered support to friends in need. When Sammy Davis Jr. lost an eye in a car accident in November 1954, Frank dedicated his time to his friend's psychological rehabilitation. When retired actor George Raft owed the IRS a large sum of money, Frank sent him a blank check. After a severe heart attack, actor Lee J. Cobb was overwhelmed with flowers, books, care, and personal attention from Frank, who even moved Cobb into his Palm Springs home and then his Los Angeles apartment. When Buddy Rich had a heart attack, Frank paid all the hospital bills. Time and again, he bailed friends out of financial jams.

Frank also helped those he did not know. The actor Bela Lugosi, whom Frank had never met, combatted heroin addiction for much of his life. On learning that Lugosi had checked into a hospital in March 1955, Frank sent him a basket of food and a note of encouragement. Lugosi later said that Frank was the only star he heard from. And there were countless times when Sinatra read a newspaper story of someone in need and sent an anonymous gift. A California priest said that he was known in show biz circles as "the world's softest touch."

Frank received many awards and commendations for his humanitarian work over the years. Among them were the following: the Jean Hersholt Humanitarian Award at the Oscars (April 15, 1971); the Friars Club's Humanitarian Award (September 23, 1972); the Medal of Valor from Israel in appreciation for his raising bond pledges for that country (November 1, 1972); the Scopus Award from the American Friends of the Hebrew University (November 14, 1976); the Freedom Medal (July 4, 1977); the Columbus Citizens Committee's Humanitarian Award (October 6, 1979); the Presidential Medal of Freedom (May 23, 1985); and the Life Achievement Award from the Los Angeles Chapter of the NAACP (May 14, 1987).

Perhaps the words of Pope Paul VI to Dolly Sinatra best summed up Frank Sinatra as a humanitarian. When Dolly had an audience with him, the Pope told her that her son was "close to God because he does God's work and does not talk about it."

My Way

Sinatra, Past and Future

"*I've lived a life that's full . . .*"

F rank Sinatra once told his daughter Nancy that he hoped to live to the year 2000. He didn't quite make it.

Nevertheless, as much as any man, he symbolized the twentieth century. With the possible exception of Elvis, Sinatra was the single most important American popular entertainer of the century. His ups and downs through all but its first two decades reflect the trials and tribulations of the modern age. His contributions to American popular music were incomparable. He created a range of movie characters reflecting the varieties of human nature. His sensibilities shaped our own. While entertaining us, he also inspired us with his flair for living, and he set a sterling example of social awareness and commitment.

Frank entered the 1990s with growing health problems and a weakened voice. Yet he remained active and made numerous concert appearances—more than two hundred through 1994. The CBS television miniseries airing in November 1992, *Sinatra: The Music Was Just the Beginning*, written and produced by Tina Sinatra, generated a lot of excitement surrounding Ol' Blue Eyes, particularly for its unflinching portrayal of his less flattering aspects. So did the album *Duets*, featuring Frank singing standards with other vocalists—Luther Vandross, Aretha Franklin, Bono of U2, Barbra Streisand, Liza Minnelli, Carly Simon, Tony Bennett, Gloria Estefan, Anita Baker, and Julio Iglesias— which was released in October 1993. In one month, it reached Number One on the *Billboard* charts. By February 1994, it had gone multiplatinum, becoming the best-selling album of Frank's career. *Duets II* followed in November 1994–with Frank Jr., Stevie Wonder, Gladys Knight, Lena Horne, Patti LaBelle, Jimmy Buffett, Willie Nelson, Neil Diamond, Antonio Carlos Jobim, Steve Lawrence, Eydie Gorme, Linda Ronstadt, Chrissie Hynde, and Lorrie Morgan. That too went multiplatinum. Both albums, in fact, outsold every other Sinatra release.

On March 1, 1994, Frank received a Grammy Legends Award for his lifetime achievements in music and his contributions to the profession. He had made more than 1800 recordings. Twenty-two of his albums had gone gold.

Five days later, on March 6, 1994, Frank collapsed while singing "My Way" at a concert at the Mosque Auditorium in Richmond, Virginia. His fans realized that an era was coming to a close—that every public appearance might just be his final one. Many of his close friends and co-workers were gone, or would be soon. Dean Martin would die the following year, on Christmas morning. Sammy Davis Jr. and Ava Gardner had passed away in 1990; Peter Lawford, in 1984.

Frank spent two hours in a Richmond hospital, then flew home to Palm Springs. He was back on stage in less than three weeks. He performed for the final time on February 25, 1995, at the Palm Desert Marriott Ballroom, to celebrate the Frank Sinatra Desert Classic golf tournament in Palm Springs. Although slowed by age, he wowed the audience. For the final encore, he performed "The Best Is Yet to Come."

On July 24-26, 1995, three tribute shows were held in New York City for the event *Carnegie Hall Celebrates the Music of Frank Sinatra*, each one with a different theme: "Songs for Swingin' Lovers," "Come Fly with Me," and "That's Life." On Frank's eightieth birthday, December 12, 1995, a star-studded celebration was held. Guest performers paying tribute to Frank included another generation's stars, among them Bob Dylan, Bruce Springsteen, Salt-N-Pepa, and Paula Abdul.

Meanwhile, in February 1995, Frank and Barbara decided to put their Palm Springs compound up for sale and live full-time at their Beverly Hills home. Reports of Frank's deteriorating health reached the public in November 1996. The following January, Frank suffered a "minor" heart attack and was rushed to Cedars-Sinai Medical Center for nine days of observation and tests. He ostensibly recovered, but he was never seen in public again. There were other visits to the hospital and other tests, but only his family, close friends, and doctors knew how sick he really was. Sinatra spent the last seventeen months of his life in a wheelchair or in bed, receiving close friends and family and spending quiet days and nights at home.

"I consider myself among the luckiest people in the world to have been able to make a career out of what I love to do—interpret wonderful music."

—Frank Sinatra

Previous spread: A typical Sinatra concert in the mid-eighties.

Right: Accepting the Pied Piper Award from ASCAP in Las Vegas, 1979.

Above: Sinatra at the rehearsal hall a few days before the 1980 presidential inauguration.

Right: An early forties glamour shot.

"*I'd like to be remembered as a man
who was as honest as he knew how to be in his life,
and as honest as he knew how to be in his work.*"

—*Frank Sinatra*

Frank died of a heart attack in the Cedars-Sinai emergency room at 10:50 p.m. on May 14, 1998, at the age of eighty-two. His three children and his wife Barbara were at his side.

That night and over the next days, fans traveled to the Sinatra home in Beverly Hills to pay their final respects to Frank Sinatra, the man and the artist. Others went to one of his three stars on the Hollywood Walk of Fame. On the East Coast, people congregated at what was once his block in Hoboken, at a plaque in front of the remains of his first home. A few days later, on Monday, May 19, some 800 grievers paid their respects at a memorial service at St. Francis Church, where Frank had been baptized eighty-two years earlier. The crowd, many of them standing outside in the street, sang "My Way" to honor Hoboken's favorite son.

The next day Sinatra's gardenia-covered casket was carried into Good Shepherd Church in Beverly Hills for a vigil that night. Generations of Hollywood's biggest stars, including Liza Minnelli, Tony Bennett, Gregory Peck, Kirk Douglas, Eydie Gorme, Mia Farrow, Milton Berle, Connie Stevens, Wayne Newton, Tom Selleck, Paul Anka, Joey Heatherton, Tim Conway, Bob Newhart, Ben Vereen, Ed McMahon, Anthony Quinn, Red Buttons, Marlo Thomas, Angie Dickinson, and others attended. A medley of Sinatra's songs was played, and Nancy Sinatra and Tony Bennett spoke before the Rosary was recited. Said Bennett, "We all fell in love, fell out of love, and fell in love again to the sound of his voice."

Left: At the funeral of Francis Albert Sinatra, pallbearers Steve Lawrence (center right), Don Rickles (third from left), and Tom Dreesen (far right) carry his coffin. Barbara Sinatra is behind Dreesen as they depart the Church of the Good Shepherd in Beverly Hills.

Next page: A heart drawn by a skywriter fills the sky over the Church of the Good Shepherd during the funeral mass.

The next day, Thursday, May 21, Francis Albert Sinatra was laid to rest at Desert Memorial Park in Palm Springs after a simple graveside ceremony. Included in his coffin, at his insistence, were ten dimes for telephone change, a pack of cigarettes, and a bottle of Jack Daniel's. He was buried next to his parents and his best friend Jilly Rizzo. Earlier that day, at his funeral at a midday mass at Good Shepherd Church, hundreds of Hollywood legends and well-wishers bade him farewell. Tony Bennett sang "Ave Maria." Gregory Peck delivered one of the eulogies, as did Sinatra's son, Frank Jr., who ended with, "So long, buddy, and take care of yourself." Applause erupted inside the church when Kirk Douglas told the 400 mourners, "Boy, heaven will never be the same." As usual, Sinatra himself had the last word, as the service ended with a recording of his forties theme song, "Put Your Dreams Away."

The outpouring of grief, remembrances, and tributes continued over the next months—from family and friends, stars and fans. The sentiment was repeated again and again—that Frank Sinatra will live on through his music, his films, and his deeds.

Forever Sinatra.

"I've been overly rewarded in my lifetime,
and that's not buttering anybody up.
I appreciate what's happened to me,
and I wish everybody . . .
thousands of times more than I've gotten in my life.
And I wish everybody in the world a lot of sweet
things, and pleasant dreams,
and soft touching, hugging, and kissing."

—Frank Sinatra

Appendix
A Sinatra Chronology

December 12, 1915 Albert Francis Sinatra is born at 415 Monroe Street in Hoboken, New Jersey, to Natalie Catherine ("Dolly") Garavente Sinatra and Anthony Martin ("Marty") Sinatra.

April 2, 1916 Frank is baptized at St. Francis Church in Hoboken (and named after his godfather Frank Garrick, an Irish newspaper man and close friend of his father).

ca. 1927 Sinatra family moves to nicer apartment on Park Avenue in Hoboken.

1928-31 Frank attends David E. Rue Junior High School in Hoboken.

1930 Fifteen-year-old Frank attends A. J. Demarest High School in Hoboken. (Most reports claim he dropped out seven weeks into his first, i.e., sophomore year.)

1930's Frank works a variety of blue-collar jobs, including helping deliver newspapers for the *Jersey Observer* in 1932, manual labor on the waterfront, and plastering.

1932 Sinatra family purchases three-story house at 841 Garden Street in Hoboken.

1932-35 Frank performs locally at school dance, weddings, roadhouses, social clubs, and political meetings.

Summer, 1934 Frank meets Nancy Carol Barbato, age 17, while living at his Aunt Josie's in Long Branch on the Jersey Shore

Summer, 1935 Frank hears idol Bing Crosby live at Loew's Journal Square in Jersey City.

September 8, 1935 Frank auditions for NBC's radio show *Major Bowes and His Original Amateur Hour,* broadcast live from the Capitol Theater in New York City. He is teamed with the Three Flashes and they perform as the Hoboken Four, singing the Mills Brothers' "Shine." (Their appearance is a success, and they play a succession of dates as part of Major Bowes' traveling show; Frank becomes the star of the entire touring unit, but returns to Hoboken after about three months.)

1935-37 Frank again works local gigs in the Hoboken region.

May 12, 1937 Frank performs swing music as Frank Sinatra and the Four Sharps on the radio show *Town Hall Tonight,* hosted by Fred Allen.

1938-39 Frank works as a singing waiter/emcee at the Rustic Cabin in Englewood, New Jersey. Once a week, the singer and the band are heard on a local radio broadcast, WNEW's *Saturday Dance Parade.*

November 26, 1938 Frank is arrested at the Rustic Cabin for breach of promise to Antoinette (Toni) Della Penta Francke. On December 22, he is charged with "committing adultery." The charge is dismissed in open court on January 24, 1939.

February 4, 1939 Frank marries Nancy Barbato.

June 1939 Harry James hears Frank sing on WNEW's *Saturday Dance Parade.* The next night, he visits the Rustic Cabin to hear him live and signs him to a two-year contract as lead vocalist in his new band, the Music Makers.

June 30, 1939 Frank makes his first appearance with Harry James and the Music Makers at the Hippodrome Theater in Baltimore.

July 1939 Frank makes his first recordings with Harry James: "Melancholy Mood" and "From the Bottom of My Heart."

December 1939 At a musicians' benefit in Chicago, bandleader Tommy Dorsey auditions Frank.

January 1940 Frank makes his first live appearances with Tommy Dorsey's band (their first documented concert together takes place in Rockford, Illinois).

February 1, 1940 Frank makes his first recordings with Tommy Dorsey: "The Sky Fell Down" and "Too Romantic."

May 23, 1940 Frank records "I'll Never Smile Again" with Dorsey; it becomes a Number One single.

June 8, 1940 Birth of Nancy Sandra Sinatra.

1941 Frank is voted Outstanding Male Vocalist in both *Billboard* and *Downbeat* magazines.

1941 Frank makes his first feature film appearances as part of Tommy Dorsey's band in *Las Vegas Nights* and *Ship Ahoy*.

December 9, 1941 Frank is classified as "4-F" at the Newark Induction Center because of a "punctured eardrum" suffered during birth.

January 19, 1942 Frank makes his first solo recording on RCA's Bluebird Records: "Night and Day," "The Night We Call It a Day," "The Song Is You," and "Lamplighter's Serenade." Dorsey arranger Axel Stordahl arranges and conducts.

September 3, 1942 Frank makes his last appearance with Tommy Dorsey.

December 30, 1942 Backed by headliner Benny Goodman, Frank makes his first solo appearance—as an "extra added attraction"—at the Paramount Theater. The show is a phenomenal success, and his four-week engagement is extended another four weeks.

February 1943 Frank makes his first feature film appearance without the Dorsey band in Columbia Pictures' *Reveille with Beverly*.

February 1943 Frank joins the popular CBS radio program *Your Hit Parade*.

March 1943 Frank signs with Columbia Records. Because of a strike by the musicians' union, he can't yet record, so Columbia re-issues "All or Nothing at All," recorded with Harry James in 1939, which becomes his first million-seller. Frank makes his first solo recordings on June 3, 1943, including "You'll Never Know," "Close to You," and "People Will Say We're in Love."

September 12, 1943 Frank signs a seven-picture deal with RKO.

December 1943 *Higher and Higher*, Frank's first RKO movie , is released—Frank's first speaking role.

January 5, 1944 *The Frank Sinatra Show* first airs on CBS radio, beginning a three-and-a-half year run.

January 10, 1944 Birth of Franklin Wayne Emmanuel (Frank Jr.) Sinatra.

February 1944 Frank signs a long-term movie contract with MGM.

Spring, 1944 The Sinatra family moves to California.

October 12, 1944 A riot breaks out on Columbus Day in Times Square in New York City when 30,000 fans mob the Paramount Theater in the hope of hearing Frank.

May-July 1945 Frank tours North Africa and Italy with the USO.

August 1945 *Anchors Away*, Frank's first MGM picture, co-starring Gene Kelly, is released.

September 1945 *The House I Live In*, a ten-minute short in which Frank speaks to a group of boys about racial and religious tolerance, is released.

March 7, 1946 *The House I Live In* earns Frank a special Oscar.

February 1947 Frank is first linked to the Mafia in newspaper reports stating he is seen in Havana with mobster Lucky Luciano.

April 8, 1947 Frank punches Hearst gossip columnist Lee Mortimer, who has been especially critical of his mob ties.

October 30, 1947 During "Frank Sinatra Day" in Hoboken, Frank is given the key to the city.

June 20, 1948 Birth of Christina (Tina) on Father's Day.

December 1949 *On the Town*, starring Frank and Gene Kelly as sailors on leave in New York City, is released.

February 14, 1950 Nancy Barbato Sinatra files for a legal separation from Frank.

April 27, 1950 MGM cancels Frank's contract.

May 27, 1950 Frank makes his television debut on Bob Hope's *Star Spangled Review*.

October 7, 1950 The CBS television variety series, *The Frank Sinatra Show*, begins a two-year run.

November 1, 1951 Frank obtains a Nevada divorce from Nancy.

November 7, 1951 Frank marries actress Ava Gardner.

June 1952 Frank is dropped by his talent agency, MCA.

September 1952 Frank makes his last recording with Columbia Records after termination of his contract.

March 1953   Frank signs with Capitol Records.

April 30, 1953   Frank is paired with arranger/ producer Nelson Riddle in a recording session for the first time. The new Sinatra sound, full of sophistication and energy, finds instant success.

August 17, 1953   *From Here to Eternity* is released; Frank receives rave reviews for his portrayal of the character Angelo Maggio.

October 1953   Frank and Ava Gardner announce their separation.

January 1954   Frank buys a two-percent interest in the Sands Hotel in Las Vegas (which later grows to nine percent and which he holds for ten years).

March 25, 1954   Frank wins the Oscar for Best Supporting Actor for *From Here To Eternity.*

November 1955   *Guys and Dolls* is released; Frank acts opposite Marlon Brando in this musical.

January 1956   *The Man With the Golden Arm* is released. Frank is later nominated for an Oscar for Best Actor, but does not win.

August 1956   *High Society* is released; Frank stars with Bing Crosby and Grace Kelly.

Spring, 1957   *Pal Joey* is released; Frank stars with Rita Hayworth and Kim Novak.

October 18, 1957   Debut of *The Frank Sinatra Show* on ABC television.

1959   Frank wins a Grammy for Best Album of the Year (*Come Dance with Me*) and Best Solo Vocal Performance ("Come Dance with Me").

1960   Frank forms Reprise Records, and makes his first recordings for the label on December 12. The first Reprise album, *Ring-a-Ding-Ding,* is released in February 1961.

May 12, 1960   Elvis Presley appears with Frank on *The Frank Sinatra-Timex Special: "Welcome Home Elvis"* on ABC Television. The special is the highest-rated TV show in years.

August 1960   The first Rat Pack movie, *Ocean's Eleven*—with Dean Martin, Sammy Davis Jr., Peter Lawford, and Joey Bishop—is released.

January 1961   Frank produces President John F. Kennedy's inaugural ball.

August 15, 1961   Frank and partners open Cal-Neva Lodge in Lake Tahoe, Nevada.

October 1962   *The Manchurian Candidate,* a Cold War psychodrama, is released; Frank gives one of his most powerful performances.

September 1963   The Nevada Gaming Control Board investigates Frank's relationship with Chicago mobster Sam Giancana, who had been a week-long guest at Frank's Cal-Neva Lodge in Lake Tahoe, and force the revocation Frank's casino gambling license. He has to sell off his interest in Cal-Neva Lodge and the Sands Hotel by January 9, 1964.

December 8, 1963   Frank Sinatra Jr. is kidnapped and held for two days.

1965   Frank wins a Grammy for Best Album of the Year (*September of My Years*) and Best Solo Vocal Performance ("It Was A Very Good Year").

July 19, 1966   Frank marries Mia Farrow.

1966   Frank wins a Grammy for Best Album of the Year (*Sinatra: A Man and his Music*) and Best Record of the Year ("Strangers in the Night").

November 1967   Frank and Mia separate.

August 16, 1968   Frank and Mia divorce.

June 1968   *The Detective* is released; Frank receives acclaim for his performance in this urban crime drama.

January 24, 1969   Frank's father Marty dies.

July 20, 1969   On the Apollo 11 mission to the moon, the astronauts beam back to earth Frank's rendition of "Fly Me to the Moon."

March 23, 1971   Frank announces his retirement from show business.

April 15, 1971   Frank receives the Jean Hersholt Humanitarian Award at the Oscars.

June 13, 1971   Frank performs his "retirement" concert at the Los Angeles Music Center.

April 30, 1973   Frank returns to the studio to record tracks for his *Ol' Blue Eyes Is Back* album; a television special of that name airs in November.

1973   Frank receives the Entertainer of the Century Award from the Songwriters of America.

May 22, 1974   Frank becomes a grandfather when daughter Nancy gives birth to Angela Jennifer Lambert. A second granddaughter, Amanda Katherine Lambert, is born March 17, 1976.

July 11, 1976   Frank marries Barbara Marx, widow of Zeppo Marx.

January 6, 1977   Frank's mother Dolly dies.

March 14, 1977   Frank participates in his final recording session with arranger/conductor Nelson Riddle: "Linda," "Sweet Lorraine," and a vocal overdub of "Barbara."

October 1980   *The First Deadly Sin* is released, Frank's first movie since retirement and his last lead role.

December 1983   Frank receives the Lifetime Achievement Award from the Kennedy Center.

January 1985   Frank produces President's Ronald Reagan inaugural ball.

May 23, 1985   Frank receives honorary degree from Stevens Institute of Technology, an engineering school in hometown of Hoboken (which his parents hoped he would attend).

November 1992   The miniseries *Sinatra: The Music Was Just the Beginning,* based on Frank's life story from 1920 to 1974 and written and produced by Tina Sinatra, airs on CBS-TV.

October 1993   The album *Duets* is released, featuring Frank singing standards with other vocalists. By November, it is Number One on the *Billboard* album chart. By February 1994, it has gone multiplatinum, and eventually sells 7 million copies, the biggest album of his career. *Duets II* follows in November 1994.

March 1, 1994   Frank receives the Grammy Legend Award for his lifetime accomplishments in music.

March 6, 1994   Frank collapses at a concert at Mosque Auditorium in Richmond, Virginia, while singing "My Way." He is treated at a local hospital and walks out three hours later.

July 24-26, 1995   In a series of three tribute concerts, *Carnegie Hall Celebrates the Music of Frank Sinatra,* various artists perform Frank's music in honor of his eightieth birthday.

October 1995   Reprise releases *The Complete Reprise Studio Recordings,* a 20-CD, 454-song boxed set of every studio recording he made for the label between 1960 and 1988.

January 1997   Frank suffers a heart attack and is rushed to Cedars-Sinai Hospital in Los Angeles.

February 1998   Frank undergoes tests at Cedars-Sinai Medical Center.

May 14, 1998   Frank Sinatra dies of a heart attack at 10:50 p.m. at Cedars-Sinai Medical Center in Los Angeles.

May 19, 1998   Generations of Hollywood stars, including Liza Minnelli, Tony Bennett, Gregory Peck, Kirk Douglas, Eydie Gorme, Mia Farrow, Milton Berle, Connie Stevens, Wayne Newton, Tom Selleck, Paul Anka, Joey Heatherton, Tim Conway, Bob Newhart, Ben Vereen, Ed McMahon, Anthony Quinn, Red Buttons, Marlo Thomas, and Angie Dickinson, gather to mourn Sinatra in an hour-long vigil held at Beverly Hills' Good Shepherd Church.

May 20, 1998   Frank Sinatra is laid to rest in Desert Memorial Park in Cathedral City Cemetery, Palm Springs, next to his parents and best friend Jilly Rizzo.

Discography

(Limited to long-playing records and CDs. Releases are long-playing records unless otherwise indicated. Thanks to Robert Urban at urbans@worldnet.att.net for his assistance.)

Columbia:

Frankie (1955)

The Voice (1955)

Frank Sinatra Conducts the Music of Alec Wilder (1956)

That Old Feeling (1956)

Adventures of the Heart (1957)

Christmas Dreaming (1957)

The Frank Sinatra Story (1958)

Put Your Dreams Away (1958)

Love is a Kick (1958)

The Broadway Kick (1959)

Come Back to Sorrento (1959)

Greatest Hits/The Early Years (1965)

Get Happy (1966)

I've Got a Crush on You (1966)

Christmas with Sinatra (1966)

The Essential Sinatra (1966)

Greatest Hits/The Early Years, Volume 2 (1967)

The Essential Frank Sinatra, Volume 1 (1967)

The Essential Frank Sinatra, Volume 2 (1967)

The Essential Frank Sinatra, Volume 3 (1967)

Frank Sinatra in Hollywood 1943-1949 (1968)

Frank Sinatra The Voice: The Columbia Years, 1943-1952 (CD, 1986)

The Best of the Columbia Years (4-CD set, 1993)

The Columbia Years: The Complete Recordings 1943-1952 (12-CD set, 1993)

Sinatra: The V-Discs (2-CD set, 1994)

Swing and Dance with Frank Sinatra (CD, 1997)

Capitol:

Songs for Young Lovers (1954)

Swing Easy (1954)

In the Wee Small Hours (1955)

High Society (1956)

Songs for Swingin' Lovers! (1956)

This is Sinatra (1956)

Frank Sinatra Conducts Tone Poems of Color (1956)

A Jolly Christmas from Frank Sinatra (1957)

A Swingin' Affair! (1957)

Close to You (1957)

Pal Joey (1957)

Where Are You? (1957)

Come Fly With Me (1958)

Only the Lonely (1958)

This Is Sinatra, Vol. 2 (1958)

Come Dance With Me! (1959)

Look to Your Heart (1959)

Nice 'n' Easy (1960)

No One Cares (1959)

Can-Can (1960)

Sinatra's Swingin' Session!!! (1960)

All the Way (1961)

Come Swing With Me! (1961)

Point of No Return (1962)

Sinatra Sings of Love and Things (1962)

Frank Sinatra Sings Rodgers and Hart (1963)

Tell Her You Love Her (1963)

The Selected Johnny Mercer (1963)

The Great Hits of Frank Sinatra (1964)

The Selected Cole Porter (1965)

Forever Frank (1966)

The Movie Songs (1967)

The Capitol Years (3-CD set, 1990)

Duets (CD, 1993)

Duets II (CD, 1994)

Sinatra 80th—Live in Concert (CD, 1995)

The Complete Capitol Singles Collection (CD, 1996)

Reprise:

Ring-a-Ding-Ding! (1961)

Sinatra Swings/Swing Along with Me (1961)

I Remember Tommy (1961)

Sinatra and Strings (1962)

Sinatra and Swingin' Brass (1962))

All Alone (1962)

The Concert Sinatra (1963)

Sinatra-Basie: An Historic Musical First (1963)

Sinatra's Sinatra (1963)

Days of Wine and Roses, Moon River, and Other Academy Award Winners (1964)

Sinatra-Basie: It Might As Well Be Swing (1964)

Softly, As I Leave You (1964)

12 Songs of Christmas (with Bing Crosby) (1964)

A Man and His Music (2-LP set) (1965)

My Kind of Broadway (1965)

Sinatra '65 (1965)

September of My Years (1965)

That's Life (1965)

Strangers in the Night (1966)

Moonlight Sinatra (1966)

Sinatra at the Sands (with Count Basie) (1966)

Francis Albert Sinatra & Antonio Carlos Jobim (1967)

The World We Knew and Frank & Nancy (1967)

Cycles (1968)

Francis A. & Edward K. (with Duke Ellington) (1968)

The Sinatra Family Wish You a Merry Christmas (1968)

Frank Sinatra's Greatest Hits (1968)

My Way (1969)

A Man Alone (1969)

Watertown (1970)

Sinatra & Company (1971)

Frank Sinatra's Greatest Hits, Vol. 2 (1972)

Ol' Blue Eyes is Back (1973)

Some Nice Things I've Missed (1974)

Sinatra The Main Event Live (1974)

Trilogy: Past, Present & Future (3-LP set) (1980)

She Shot Me Down (1981)

The Reprise Collection (4-CD set, 1990)

Sinatra Reprise—The Very Good Years (CD, 1991)

Frank Sinatra and Sextet: Live in Paris (1962 recording) (CD, 1994)

The Sinatra Christmas Album (CD, 1994)

The Complete Reprise Studio Recordings (20-CD set, 1995)

Everything Happens to Me (CD, 1996)

Warner Bros.:

Sinatra Sings Great Songs from Great Britain (1962)

Qwest:

L.A. Is My Lady (1984)

BMG/RCA:

Tommy Dorsey-Frank Sinatra: The Song Is You (5-CD set, 1994)

Frank Sinatra & Tommy Dorsey Greatest Hits (CD, 1996)

Frank Sinatra and the Tommy Dorsey Orchestra: Love Songs (CD, 1997)

Sony:

Frank Sinatra Conducts the Music of Alec Wilder (CD, 1956)

Christmas Songs by Frank Sinatra (CD, 1994)

Sinatra Sings Rodgers and Hammerstein (CD, 1996)

Portrait of Sinatra: Columbia Classics (2-CD set, 1997)

Frank Sinatra Sings His Greatest Hits (CD, 1997)

Blue Note:

Frank Sinatra with the Red Norvo Quintet: Live in *Australia, 1959* (CD, 1997)

Filmography

Major Bowes' Amateur Theatre of the Air (1935, RKO)

Las Vegas Nights (1941, Paramount)

Ship Ahoy (1942, MGM)

Reveille with Beverly (1943, Columbia)

Higher and Higher (1943, RKO)

Step Lively (1944, RKO)

Anchors Aweigh (1945, MGM)

The House I Live In (1945, RKO)

Till the Clouds Roll By (1946, MGM)

It Happened in Brooklyn (1947, MGM)

The Miracle of the Bells (1948, RKO)

The Kissing Bandit (1948, MGM)

Take Me Out to the Ball Game (1949, MGM)

On the Town (1949, MGM)

Double Dynamite (1951, RKO)

Meet Danny Wilson (1951, Universal-International)

From Here to Eternity (1953, Columbia)

Suddenly (1954, United Artists)

Young at Heart (1954, Warner Brothers)

Not As a Stranger (1955, United Artists)

The Tender Trap (1955, MGM)

Guys and Dolls (1955, MGM)

The Man with the Golden Arm (1955, United Artists)

Meet Me in Las Vegas (1956, MGM)

Johnny Concho (1956, United Artists)

High Society (1956, MGM)

Around the World in Eighty Days (1956, United Artists)

The Pride and the Passion (1957, United Artists)

The Joker is Wild (1957, Paramount)

Pal Joey (1957, Columbia)

Kings Go Forth (1958, United Artists)

Some Came Running (1958, MGM)

A Hole in the Head (1959, United Artists)

Never So Few (1959, MGM)

Can-Can (1960, Twentieth Century-Fox)

Ocean's Eleven (1960, Warner Brothers)

Pepe (1960, Columbia)

The Devil at Four O'Clock (1961, Columbia)

Sergeants 3 (1962, United Artists)

The Road to Hong Kong (1962, United Artists)

The Manchurian Candidate (1962, United Artists)

Come Blow Your Horn (1963, Paramount)

The List of Adrian Messenger (1963, Universal)

4 for Texas (1964, Warner Brothers)

Robin and the Seven Hoods (1964, Warner Brothers)

None But the Brave (1965, Warner Brothers)

Von Ryan's Express (1965, Twentieth Century-Fox)

Marriage on the Rocks (1965, Warner Brothers)

Cast a Giant Shadow (1965, United Artists)

The Oscar (1966, Embassy)

Assault on a Queen (1966, Paramount)

The Naked Runner (1967, Warner Brothers)

Tony Rome (1967, Twentieth Century-Fox)

The Detective (1968, Twentieth Century-Fox)

Lady in Cement (1968, Twentieth Century-Fox)

Dirty Dingus Magee (1970, MGM)

That's Entertainment (1974, MGM)

That's Entertainment, Part II (1976, MGM)

Contract on Cherry Street (1977, Columbia) (Made for TV)

The First Deadly Sin (1980, Filmways/Artanis/Cinema Seven)

Cannonball Run II (1984, Warner Brothers)

Who Framed Roger Rabbit? (1988, Warner Brothers/Touchstone/Amblin)

Listen Up: The Lives of Quincy Jones (1991, Warner Brothers/Cort)

The Films of John Frankenheimer (1995)

Sinatra: 80 Years My Way (1995)

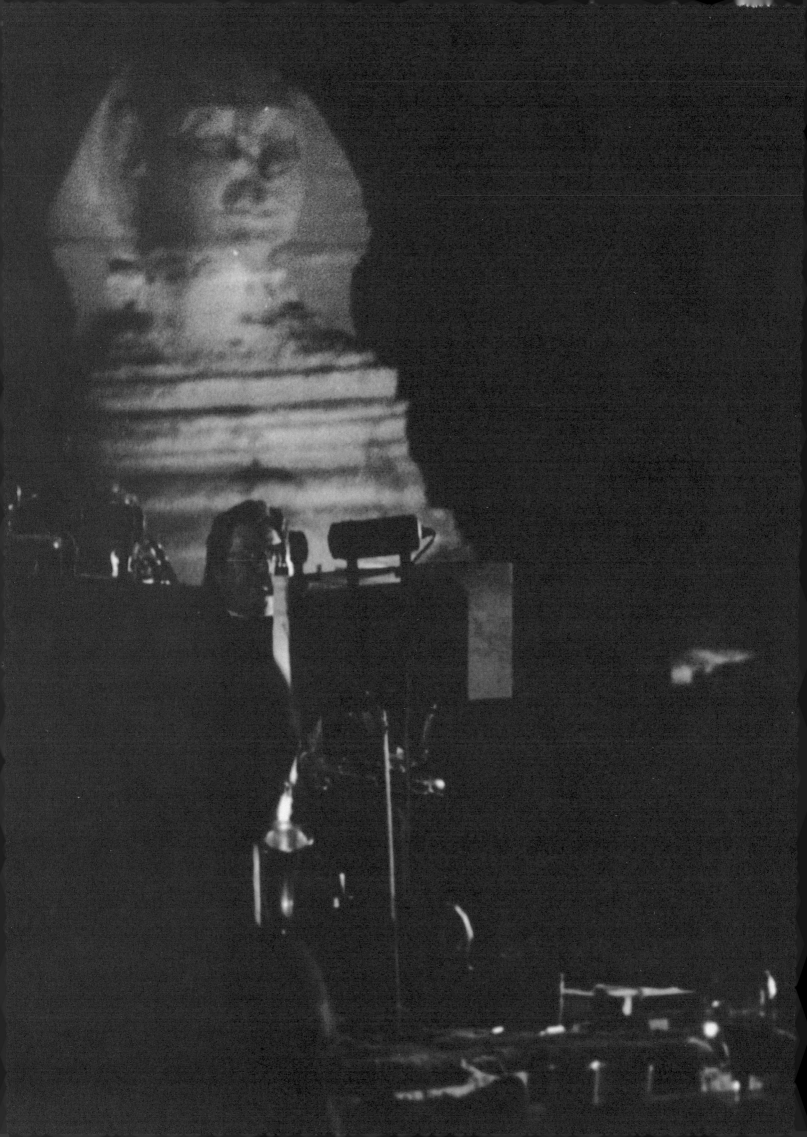